*When Allah willed to create the horse, He said to the South Wind,
"I will that a creature should proceed from thee — condense thyself!"
And the wind condensed itself.*

Emir Abd-El-Kader
1807-1883
Letter to General E. Daumas, 1857

The Greatest Horse of All
A Controversy Examined

by

Charles Justice

authorHOUSE®

AuthorHouse™
1663 Liberty Drive, Suite 200
Bloomington, IN 47403
www.authorhouse.com
Phone: 1-800-839-8640

First published by AuthorHouse 11/17/2008

ISBN: 978-1-4389-0193-0 (sc)
ISBN: 978-1-4389-0192-3 (hc)

Library of Congress Control Number: 2008906867

Printed in the United States of America
Bloomington, Indiana

This book is printed on acid-free paper.

All scriptural quotations are from The Jerusalem Bible, copyright 1992

DEDICATION

In loving memory of my mother,

ELEANOR REID JUSTICE

1916-2006

ACKNOWLEDGMENTS

The following people helped bring this book to completion and are gratefully acknowledged:

Mr. Adam S. Beaver, Bloomington, Indiana: provided cover design and graphics layout.

Mr. Allan Carter, Historian of the National Museum of Racing and Hall of Fame, Saratoga Springs, New York: provided copies of Optimistic Gal's past performance records.

Mr. Adam Coglianese, Official Track Photographer, New York Racing Association: provided the cover photographs.

Mr. J. Michael Hopkins, Director of the Maryland Racing Commission: confirmed Secretariat's officially accepted Preakness time.

Mrs. Ann M. Justice: suggested the stopwatch image as part of the jacket design.

Mr. Donald Kapper, Progressive Nutrition, Beach City, Ohio: provided expertise regarding equine nutrition in the early twentieth century.

Mr. Richard Sowers: critiqued the original manuscript and made key suggestions for improvements.

Mr. Matt Wooley, EquiSportPhotos.com: provided the frontispiece photograph of Street Sense with Calvin Borel.

PREFACE

THE GREATEST HORSE OF ALL:
A CONTROVERSY EXAMINED

I began this book in early November 2006 while sitting at the foot of my mother's bed. She was then in a nursing facility in Columbus, Indiana.

I realized that she would never be able to read the book, nor even to know that I wrote it, but I resolved to write it based on the principles she taught me throughout life – with as much honesty and integrity as I possibly could.

The subject itself, obviously, fascinated me. I've always loved controversies!

The finished product, in every sense, thus bears an invisible and yet indelible stamp of her character, a reflection of her humor and intelligence, as I absorbed those traits over the sixty-four years we interacted.

My mother, I readily admit, was my greatest teacher. I said this at her eulogy, and it bears repeating.

She was one of those immensely talented people – a brilliant pianist – who become, much like the unrecognized in Thomas Gray's *Elegy in a Country Churchyard,* an "ordinary" wage earner and homemaker – and thus the true foundation of whatever is good and noble in this country.

My mother loved nature and all its creatures. She especially liked to watch horses run. At times during writing, when I seemed stuck and needing an apt expression, a thought would suddenly surface concerning what seemed the inexplicably correct phrasing.

I have no doubt that my mother was communicating with me in a special way at those times.

Thanks, Mom. As ever, I owe you more than I can repay. I hope you enjoy the book.

Charles J. Justice
Bloomington, Indiana
February 22, 2008

CONTENTS

INTRODUCTION

Methods of Study

This book is about selecting a candidate for greatest Thoroughbred racehorse of the twentieth century based on criteria stated below.

It cannot claim absolute selection of the greatest horse of all time mainly because records are unavailable, or were never completely documented, on all horses qualifying as Thoroughbreds since the breed developed.

Some argue that a valid selection is impossible, but they unhesitatingly accept the ranking presented, for example, in the 1999 Blood-Horse publication (hereafter BHI) entitled *Thoroughbred Champions: Top 100 Racehorses of the 20th Century*. (1)

They apparently don't realize that such rankings imply both comparison and selection. Or, more likely, they accept the ranking because their favorite horse was chosen as greatest.

In contrast to subjective choices, this book uses basic statistical comparisons for making selections. However, this emphatically *is not* a statistics text. It uses practical or applied statistics to compare, rank and select among racing records, and it explains each step of those rankings for the reader as it proceeds.

Contrary to popular opinion, statistics is not a boring, esoteric or lame subject. It has been maligned greatly because it has often been applied inappropriately. Such application will be avoided herein.

The only mathematical background one needs to understand basic statistical conclusions is familiarity with the common operations of addition, subtraction, multiplication and division – plus finding squares and square roots. The latter are reviewed herein.

The data used by the author to select the candidate greatest Thoroughbred(s) are, with the exceptions of Optimistic Gal, Phar Lap and Kincsem, included in the 2000 publication by the Daily Racing Form entitled *Champions*.(2) This publication will hereafter be referenced as DRFC.

Forty-four BHI horses were chosen for statistical comparison. Their BHI rankings ranged from 1 to 76. Six additional horses were included in at least one level of the study. They were recommended by Richard Sowers, author of *The Abstract Primer of Thoroughbred Racing*.(3) A total of fifty horses were thus included in this study.

Excursus A lists the top 100 BHI horses, including brief vital statistics. Those from the BHI list included in this study are highlighted in the Excursus. The six recommended horses are listed separately.

Excursus A
Top 100 Blood-Horse Champions

Horse*	Birth Year	BHI Rank	Ages Raced	Record**
Man o' War-c	1917	1+	2,3	21-20-1-0
Secretariat-c	1970	2	2,3	21-16-3-1
Citation-c	1945	3	2,3,5,6	45-32-10-2
Kelso-g	1957	4	2 thru 9	63-39-12-2
Count Fleet-c	1940	5	2,3	21-16-4-1
Dr. Fager-c	1964	6	2,3,4	22-18-2-1
Native Dancer-c	1950	7	2,3,4	22-21-1-0
Forego-g	1970	8	3 thru 8	57-34-9-7
Seattle Slew-c	1974	9	2,3,4	17-14-2-0
Spectacular Bid-c	1976	10	2,3,4	30-26-2-1
Tom Fool-c	1949	11	2,3,4	30-21-7-1
Affirmed-c	1975	12	2,3,4	29-22-5-1
War Admiral-c	1934	13	2,3,4,5	26-21-3-1
Buckpasser-c	1963	14	2,3,4	31-25-4-1
Colin-c	1905	15	2,3	15-15-0-0
Damascus-c	1964	16	2,3,4	32-21-7-3

Round Table-c	1954	17	2,3,4,5	66-43-8-5
Cigar-c	1990	18	3,4,5,6	33-19-4-5
Bold Ruler-c	1954	19	2,3,4	33-23-4-2
Swaps-c	1952	20	2,3,4	25-19-2-2
Equipoise-c	1928	21	2 thru 7	51-29-10-4
Phar Lap-g	1926	22	2 thru 6	51-37-3-2
John Henry-g	1975	23	2 thru 9	83-39-15-9
Nashua-c	1952	24	2,3,4	30-22-4-1
Seabiscuit-c	1933	25	2 thru 7	89-33-15-13
Whirlaway-c	1938	26	2,3,4,5	60-32-15-9
Alydar-c	1975	27	2,3,4	26-14-9-1
Gallant Fox-c	1927	28	2,3	17-11-3-2
Exterminator-g	1915	29	2 thru 9	100-50-17-17
Sysonby-c	1902	30	2,3	15-14-0-1
Sunday Silence-c	1986	31	2,3,4	14-9-5-0
Skip Away-c	1993	32	2,3,4,5	38-18-10-6
Assault-c	1943	33	2 thru 7	42-18-6-7
Easy Goer-c	1986	34	2,3,4	20-14-5-1
Ruffian-f	1972	35	2,3	11-10-0-0
Gallant Man-c	1954	36	2,3,4	26-14-4-1
Discovery-c	1931	37	2,3,4,5	63-27-10-10
Challedon-c	1936	38	2 thru 6	44-20-7-6
Armed-g	1941	39	3 thru 9	81-41-20-10
Busher-f	1942	40	2,3,4,5	21-15-3-1
Stymie-c	1941	41	2 thru 8	131-35-33-28
Alysheba-c	1984	42	2,3,4	26-11-8-2
Northern Dancer-c	1961	43	2,3	18-14-2-2
Ack Ack-c	1966	44	2,3,4,5	27-19-6-0
Gallorette-f	1942	45	2 thru 6	72-21-20-13
Majestic Prince-c	1966	46	2,3	10-9-1-0
Coaltown-c	1945	47	3,4,5,6	39-23-6-3
Personal Ensign-f	1984	48	2,3,4	13-13-0-0
Sir Barton-c	1916	49	2,3,4	31-13-6-5

Dahlia-f	1970	50	2 thru 6	48-15-3-7
Susan's Girl-f	1969	51	2 thru 6	63-29-14-11
Twenty Grand-c	1928	52	2 thru 7	25-14-4-3
Sword Dancer-c	1956	53	2,3,4	39-15-7-4
Grey Lag-c	1918	54	2 thru 13	47-25-9-6
Devil Diver-c	1939	55	2 thru 6	47-22-12-3
Zev-c	1920	56	2,3,4	43-23-8-5
Riva Ridge-c	1969	57	2,3,4	30-17-3-1
Slew o' Gold-c	1980	58	2,3,4	21-12-5-1
Twilight Tear-f	1941	59	2,3,4	24-18-2-2
Native Diver-c	1959	60	2 thru 8	81-37-7-12
Omaha-c	1932	61	2,3,4	22-9-7-2
Cicada-f	1959	62	2,3,4,5	42-23-8-6
Silver Charm-c	1994	63	2,3,4,5	24-12-7-2
Holy Bull-c	1991	64	2,3,4	16-13-0-0
Alsab-c	1939	65	2,3,4,5	51-25-11-5
Top Flight-f	1929	66	2,3	16-12-0-0
Arts and Letters-c	1966	67	2,3,4	23-11-6-1
All Along-f	1979	68	2,3,4,5	21-9-4-2
Noor-c	1945	69	2,3,4,5	31-12-6-6
Shuvee-f	1966	70	2,3,4,5	44-16-10-6
Regret-f	1912	71	2,3,4,5	11-9-1-0
Go for Wand-f	1987	72	2,3	13-10-2-0
Johnstown-c	1936	73	2,3	21-14-0-3
Bald Eagle-c	1955	74	2,3,4,5	29-12-5-4
Hill Prince-c	1947	75	2,3,4,5	30-17-5-4
Lady's Secret-f	1982	76	2,3,4,5	45-25-9-3
Two Lea-f	1946	77	2 thru 6	26-15-6-3
Eight Thirty-c	1936	78	2,3,4,5	27-16-3-5
Gallant Bloom-f	1966	79	2,3,4	22-16-1-1
Ta Wee-f	1966	80	2,3,4	21-15-2-1
Affectionately-f	1960	81	2,3,4,5	52-28-8-6
Miesque-f	1984	82	2,3,4	16-12-3-1

Carry Back-c	1958	83	2,3,4,5	62-21-11-11
Bimelech-c	1937	84	2,3,4	15-11-2-1
Lure-c	1989	85	2,3,4,5	25-14-8-0
Fort Marcy-g	1964	86	2 thru 7	75-21-18-14
Gamely-f	1964	87	3,4,5	41-16-9-6
Old Rosebud-g	1911	88	2 thru 11	80-40-13-8
Bewitch-f	1945	89	2 thru 6	55-20-10-11
Davona Dale-f	1976	90	2,3,4	18-11-2-1
Genuine Risk-f	1977	91	2,3,4	15-10-3-2
Sarazen-g	1921	92	2 thru 7	55-27-2-6
Sun Beau-c	1925	93	2 thru 6	74-33-12-10
Artful-f	1902	94	2,3	8-6-2-0
Bayakoa-f	1984	95	2 thru 7	39-21-9-0
Exceller-c	1973	96	2 thru 6	33-15-5-6
Foolish Pleasure-c	1972	97	2,3,4	26-16-4-3
Beldame-f	1901	98	2,3,4	31-17-6-4
Roamer-g	1911	99	2 thru 8	98-39-26-9
Blue Larkspur-c	1926	100	2,3,4	16-10-3-1

* c – colt; g – gelding; f – filly
** total races-wins-places-shows
+ Column 3 shading means inclusion in present study

Horses for Special Consideration

Horse	Birth Year	Ages Raced	Record
Kincsem-f	1874	2,3,4,5	54-54-0-0
First Flight-f	1944	2,3,4	24-11-3-3
Landaluce-f	1980	2	5-5-0-0
La Prevoyante-f	1970	2,3,4	39-25-5-3
Optimistic Gal-f	1973	2,3	21-13-5-3
Noor-c	1945	2,3,4,5	31-12-6-6

These fifty horses comprise what is considered a large sample in statistical terms. By definition, a large sample has thirty or more data items.

There is thus a low probability that one of the unselected horses from the lower BHI rankings was actually better than one of the fifty selected horses. This is not saying that other horses from other countries outside North America might not have been equal or better. Rather, it is an attempt to make data handling manageable and to settle arguments within the basic purview of the BHI rankings.

The method used herein to determine the candidate greatest Thoroughbred(s) may be visualized as a three-level sieve. The following diagram illustrates this concept.

Figure I1
The Three-Level Data Filtering Process

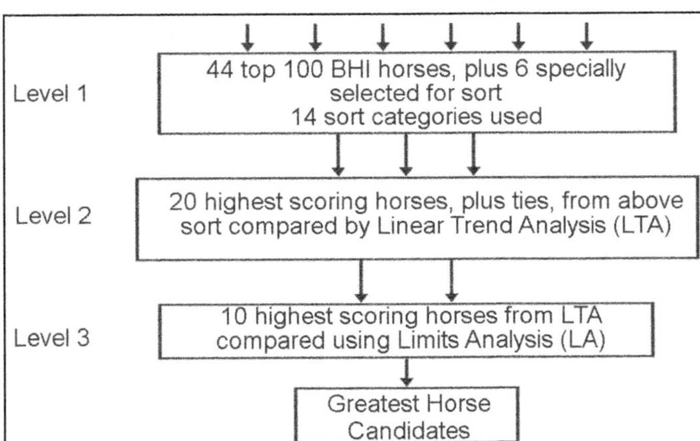

Each level in Figure I1 is explained in the text as it is applied to data. The scoring system for all levels is also explained, but is now briefly previewed.

Level 1 was a basic data sort. It was applied to the two- and three-year-old horses and consisted of fourteen sort categories by which the horses were compared. Not all horses raced at age two, and Kincsem could not be included due to incomplete data.

The first category, for example, was Average Distance Run. The process followed for sorting that category was applied separately to each of the fourteen categories for each horse. Colts and fillies were sorted together and later separated.

Two major sorts were performed. The first was on the two-year-olds' (2YO) data; the second was on the 3YO data.

Thoroughbreds must be compared in separate age and sex categories because they do not fully mature until age five (3), and because fillies generally differ from colts in strength and stamina.

That is the first rule for validly comparing Thoroughbred data, and the sorts followed it.

Each sort category either contained data given in the DRFC book (termed "raw data" by statisticians), or it represented data derived directly from raw data by a standard mathematical operation. No manipulations or transformation of data were applied to any calculations herein. Nothing was changed.

It would be pointless to spend many hours analyzing data while simultaneously knowing those data were bogus because they were manipulated to favor one horse over another – to bias the outcome. This book simply does not do that.

The above being clearly stated, we proceed to a description of the sort categories and their scoring.

Preliminary Discussion – Average Distance Run

Beginning with the 2YOs, the distance run in each race by each horse was entered in decimal format into an Excel spreadsheet file. Each 2YO typically ran ten or more races for that year (a few did not); therefore, about 400 distances were entered for this category.

For 2YOs these distances typically ranged from 5 f (0.625 miles) to 8.5 f (1.0625 miles); a furlong (1 f) is one-eighth of a statute mile, or 660 ft.

The distances each horse ran were added and then divided by their total number to obtain the average distance each 2YO ran for his or her juvenile year. These average distances were then sorted from high to low.

The justification for this category is that horses running longer average distances, and scoring higher on other related categories, deserve more credit than those averaging less distance per race.

Horses were assigned total sort points, for each category, equaling the number of horses being compared. For this study, forty-four BHI 2YO and 3YO horses were compared. Thus, the horse or horses averaging the greatest distance run per race received forty-four points, and similarly down to one point for the horse running the shortest average distance.

Average distance run is an obvious measure and needs no further explanation. The second sort category, average speed, is a bit more involved and is now explained in detail.

Preliminary Discussion – Average Speed

To start each reader on equal grounds, average speed is not given per se in the DRFC performance lines. It is, therefore, a derived criterion that is easily calculated.

Using the traditional formula: distance = speed x time (d = s x t), the distance for each race was first converted from miles (mi) to feet (ft) and was then divided by the total time in seconds (s) it took the horse to run it.

All average speeds calculated this way have units of feet per second, abbreviated hereafter as ft/s in accord with accepted scientific notation.

Calculations were done in these units because it is much easier and more meaningful to visualize a horse running so many feet per second rather than so many miles per hour.

In Thoroughbred racing, unlike at the Indy 500, one can more vividly grasp a horse running 60 ft/s versus 41 mi/hr because 60 ft/s would carry it from the pitcher's mound to home plate on a standard baseball diamond in about one second.

An easy way to convert from ft/s to mi/hr, if desired, is to recall that 60 mi/hr equals 88 ft/s. Then express the horse's speed as a fraction with 88 in the denominator and multiply by 60. The result will be his speed in mi/hr.

For example, 55 ft/s = (55 ÷ 88) x 60 = 0.625 x 60 = 37.5 mi/hr.

When all the average speeds were determined, they were then ranked from high to low, just as for average distance run, using Excel's SORT command – a very valuable tool for studies such as this.

Average speeds were also assigned sort points ranging from forty-four for the highest to one for the slowest. In cases of ties, each horse was given the same point value. No fractional points were assigned, as some studies do.

The total points for all fourteen categories, for all the 2YO horses, were similarly calculated and then ranked from high to low using a second cumulative sort.

The top twenty horses (plus ties when applicable) from the Level-1 sort then advanced to the second level of data analysis – Linear Trend Analysis, or LTA.

The remaining horses were no longer candidates for greatest horse at the 2YO level. However, their 3YO racing data, if they raced at age three, was used for that age category. They were, therefore, still viable candidates for greatest horse at the higher age level.

The data of the top ten horses (plus ties) from LTA were then compared using what is called Three-Sigma Analysis or Limits Analysis (TSA or LA). This process is straightforward and is explained later, as is LTA.

Finally, the horse(s) emerging from the LTA and TSA levels with the highest overall point total was selected as candidate for greatest North American 2YO of the twentieth century – based on the BHI rankings and the records of six recommended horses.

The same three-part process – sort, LTA and TSA – was then repeated for the 3YOs.

The discerning reader will have by now realized that one cannot summarily state that a horse is a candidate for being *the greatest* of all time – unless he or she happens to win each separate age category, and similarly for gender category.

❧

If someone approached you and claimed to have the greatest racehorse of all time, the first thing you might ask would be how many, and which, races he had won.

If the answer was that he had won none but that he didn't need to because his owner simply knew he was the greatest by watching him, you might stare in disbelief and ponder the person's sanity.

The blunt fact of racing life is that horses must prove their worth. They must run measured distances while being timed by an accurately calibrated chronometer which indicates "how long" it took to run the distance – essentially what fraction of 360 degrees the earth turned while the running occurred.

Whatever greatness truly is in a racehorse ultimately depends in some way or another on the relationship between traversing a measured distance and stopping a chronometer. It's that basic.

Can a single horse, particularly from the BHI listing, rightly claim to have done this more often and better than others? That is the question this book attempts to answer with as little bias and prejudice as possible.

CHAPTER 1

The Greatest Horse of All: Opinions

In 1999 The Blood-Horse, Inc. (BHI) issued a publication titled, "Thoroughbred Champions: Top 100 Racehorses of the 20th Century." (1)

Their choices ranged from Man o' War as number one to Blue Larkspur as number 100. Their ranking caused increased debate and some animosity between various Thoroughbred racing fans who favored a different order.

In particular, the debate and diatribes which followed became especially bitter between the advocates of Man o' War and his primary rival of fifty-three years later, Secretariat.

Secretariat was rated number two by the BHI voters.

In reading the pro-or-con arguments for one of these great Thoroughbreds versus the other, particularly from Internet sites defending their favorite champion as though the world's fate hung on the result, it was obvious that tons of emotions were being vented but scarcely an ounce of logic supported these harangues.

The acrimony of the statements reinforced the notion that the human psyche seems to contain an inherent impulse to seek and align itself with greatness in every imaginable endeavor, whatever the term actually means or implies.

The urge toward this alignment and identification is apparently as old as civilization itself, and it follows no boundaries regarding propriety.

For example, in his book *The Gifts of the Jews*, (4) Thomas Cahill notes public debates among Sumerian school children from about 5,000 years ago. During these debates, the children challenged and maligned each other regarding who was the better student!

Granted that such pride is sorely lacking today, this reinforces the notion that people are often driven to associate with greatness on any level, particularly if they are not themselves judged great.

Considerations Regarding Greatness

What, exactly, does greatness in a Thoroughbred imply? A typical dictionary definition includes descriptors such as: of extra-ordinary powers; having unusual merit; very skillful or expert (5). There seems nothing enlightening here.

Further thought convinces us, however, that greatness is both conceptually elusive and impossible to frame verbally. It is exactly like all abstract concepts such as honor, beauty, goodness and truth in this regard.

Besides the verbal definition problem, there are subtle implications regarding time, location, age and sex that are assumed when discussing Thoroughbred greatness.

The above is true because what people are generally implying when they debate the greatness of horse A versus horse B is that they have subconsciously narrowed their field of definition to a three-year-old colt(male)running on various tracks in the contiguous forty-eight American states, sometime after 1900. Their subconscious motivation is driven mainly by Triple Crown notoriety.

Clarification of Interpretations

The three-year-old is the prime focus of most racing fans because the Triple Crown races in the United States -- the Kentucky Derby, the Preakness and the Belmont, are open only to horses during their three-year-old, or sophomore, year.

These races are now considered a kind of Holy Grail of the sport, and only eleven horses have won all three since they were given the collective name *Triple Crown*. That was in 1935 when Omaha won them.

Only nine horses have actually won an *established* Triple Crown. Prior to this triad being named, Sir Barton won the first of these triplets in 1919, and Gallant Fox won the second in 1930. Omaha, the 1935 winner, was a son of Gallant Fox. Thus, Sir Barton and Gallant Fox won their Triple Crowns prior to the fact.

Of the BHI top-100 list, however, eighty-six horses raced in their fourth year and beyond, not just as two- or three-year-olds. In fact, Cigar and Forego did not race during their two-year-old (juvenile) season. One horse, Grey Lag, raced until age 13.

Thus, either unintentionally or deliberately assuming only three-year-old horses are worthy of greatness unjustly eliminates many horses from the honor and denies facts.

It is accepted wisdom among horsemen that a Thoroughbred is not mature until, by definition and physiological development, the beginning of the fifth year after its birth (3).

Many Thoroughbreds accomplish more at age four and older than at ages two or three. The excellent Australian horse, Phar Lap, is a prime example. He was ranked twenty-second by BHI voters. He won just one of five races at age two but then won thirty-five of forty-five until his untimely death. (6)

Limitations of the Study

For immediate clarification, all Thoroughbreds at birth are called foals. A male foal is a colt until age five; a female foal is a filly until age five. At age five, a colt becomes a horse (yes, this sounds a bit like double-talk) and a filly becomes a mare.

To simplify future descriptions, the generic term "horse" will be used henceforth in this book, age or sex notwithstanding.

It happens that the two highest ranked BHI horses, Man o' War and Secretariat, over which much heated debate has arisen, only raced as two- and three-year-olds.

Each, in fact, had only twenty-one total career races on which their entire reputations rest. Man o' War raced ten times during his juvenile year and eleven times during his sophomore year. Secretariat ran nine times during his juvenile and twelve times during his sophomore year.

This highlights a second point that must be considered in any serious study of Thoroughbred greatness. That is, the twenty-one total races of each of these horses – and similar numbers of races for many horses in the BHI top-100 listing – technically do not constitute a large statistical sample. Excursus A shows that fifty of the top 100 horses did not run thirty races in their entire careers. Samples of thirty or more are generally considered large for statistical purposes.

This means that one must be wary of drawing conclusions about greatness from relatively small samples. Valid conclusions can be drawn from such samples, and the purpose of this book is to discover and clearly state them. However, one must be careful not to misuse statistical methods — which already connote chicanery to some.

We must constantly strive to prevent the statement attributed to British Prime Minister Benjamin Disraeli from becoming a kind of self-fulfilling indictment – that there are three kinds of lies – lies, damned lies and statistics!

Chart 1 following shows the number of top-100 BHI-ranked horses that raced to given ages.

CHART 1
Number of top 100 horses and oldest age at which they ran.

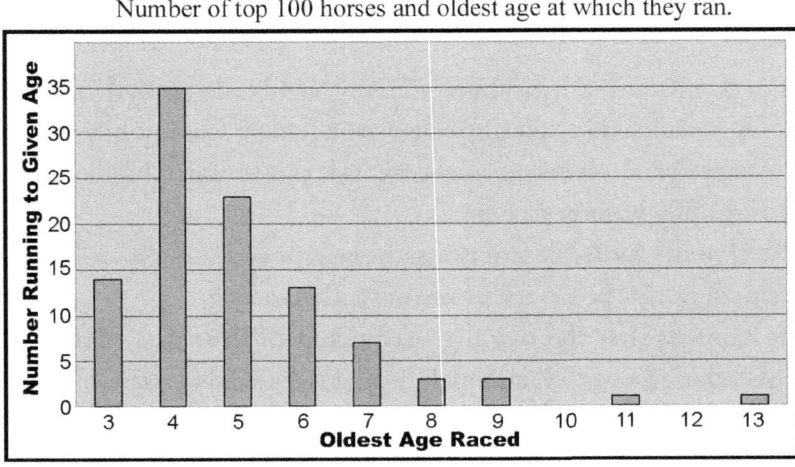

Since a colt or filly is considered immature until age five, does this imply that he or she would run better in terms of speed, consistency or ability to carry weight, than, say, during their juvenile (second) or sophomore (third) year of age?

A sample of ten of the thirteen top horses from the BHI listing partly answers this question. Of these horses, eight ran at least one faster time for the same listed distance and track condition than they did when younger.

Table 1 gives the name, age, distance, times and weights carried for ten horses, as compared with their performance at the same distance when they were three years old. The fastest times are in bold font.

Table 1
Comparison of Thoroughbred Times for
Different Ages and same Distance

Horse	Age (years)	Distance (miles)	Time (seconds)	Weight Carried (pounds)
Kelso b. 1957	3	1.0	**94.2**	117
		1.0	94.8	121
	4	1.0	95.6	130
	5	1.0	95.6	117
Dr. Fager b. 1964	3	1.0	95.2	122
			93.8	126
			96.0	120
	4	1.0	**92.2**	134
Native Dancer b. 1950	3	1.0	96.2	126
	4	1.0	**95.2**	130
Tom Fool b. 1949	3	1.0	96.4	126
			97.0	120
	4	1.0	97.2	126
			95.8	130
			96.8	126

Table 1 – continued

Citation b. 1945	3	1.125	109.0 108.8 109.2	126 126 119
	5	1.125	**106.8**	128
	6	1.125	108.4	123
Seattle Slew b. 1974	3	1.125	107.4 109.6	122 126
	4	1.125	108.0 **105.8** 107.4	128 128 134
Spectacular Bid b. 1976	3	1.125	110.0 108.8 106.6 108.4	121 122 124 122
	4	1.125	106.2 108.0 108.0 **105.8**	130 126 132 130
Forego b. 1970	3	1.25	121.0	126
	4	1.25	**119.8** 121.2 121.6	127 129 131
	5	1.25	**119.8** 121.8 120.0	132 131 129
Affirmed b. 1975	3	1.25	121.2 122.0	126 126
	4	1.25	121.0 118.6 **118.4** 121.6	126 128 132 126
War Admiral b. 1934	3	1.25	124.8 **123.2**	126 126
	4	1.25	123.8 123.8	130 126

The distances in Table 1 were chosen because each of these horses ran one or more races in multiple years at the given distance. This does not always happen due to the small number of total races generally run during a Thoroughbred's career.

The results simply reflect the fact that many horses do not run a large number of races (from a statistical standpoint) in any given year and do not necessarily repeat the same distance. This fact must be remembered because it is crucial to the type of data analysis used in this study.

For instance, it is not unusual for a horse to run two one-mile races as a three-year-old but not run that same distance at age four or older. This fact places additional limitations on valid statistical comparisons.

Accurate statistical arguments, however, can only be made by comparing same-age and/or same-gender horses at equal distances under equal track conditions, as far as practical.

Even then, one must assume that track descriptors like *fast* or *good* mean nearly the same from track to track and from one time to another. We know this isn't strictly true. However, since it is impossible to rate track conditions scientifically, we do the best comparisons reasonable. Otherwise, nothing valid could be said. The limitations of such approximations will be discussed thoroughly later in the text.

It should be evident, from the above considerations, that even a precise mathematical technique like statistics must be used circumspectly regarding Thoroughbred data analyses. Therefore, how valid are purely emotional statements about a horse's quality based simply on gut-level responses to something one likes about the creature?

Was it true, for instance, that Spectacular Bid (rated tenth by BHI) was ". . . the greatest horse ever to look through a bridle . . .," as his trainer, Grover (Bud) Delp, once claimed? (1)

Could Count Fleet (BHI rating five) really have "run down" Man o' War (BHI rating 1), as his Hall of Fame trainer Sylvester Veitch boasted? (1)

Was Hall of Fame trainer, Hollie Hughes, speaking accurately when he told jockey Ron Turcotte just before the 1973 Belmont that he couldn't get beat because he was riding the greatest horse of all time (referring, of course, to Secretariat, rated second by BHI) and that he'd seen them all? (1)

How plausible was Francis Dunne's statement when asked which was the greatest horse he'd ever seen, Man o' War or Secretariat, he answered, "Neither. I saw Phar Lap." (BHI rating twenty-two) (1)

Such accolades give but a small sample of the impact these horses had on men familiar with equine greatness and somewhat jaded by their vast exposure to its presence.

If seasoned track veterans become hyperbolic in their praise of favorite steeds, how much greater is the tendency for casual fans to exclaim, throwing all caution aside, that one horse is the greatest simply because they've heard stories of his greatness handed down through the family or have allowed the often extravagant prose of journalists to seize their imaginations and weave a mythical aura around their champion?

Even the seven BHI panelists who voted the top 100 horses of the twentieth century saw fit to allow one of their own to write a cautionary foreword.

As William Nack stated therein, "For all the work and dreaming that went into it . . . one approaches the list . . . with a nagging sense of its folly as a rational exercise and of the maddening arbitrariness of its outcome."(1)

This book's purpose is to select a candidate greatest horse or horses based upon objective reasoning, as embodied in valid, unadorned and limited statistical comparisons among data the horses and their jockeys collaborated to produce.

When all is said and done, the numbers left on paper by the past champions are *the only real facts* we can know about them. Right or wrong, they must be judged mainly by these numbers.

Anecdotal comments are worthy of consideration, but they can only be used cautiously as adjuncts to the statistics the horses produced by their performances.

Statistics, invaluable as they are, will not, however, be used so much herein that they will put readers to sleep. This book is not intended as a statistics text or primer but a tool for explaining and clarifying one topic.

In essence, it poses the question it then seeks to answer: Is it possible for basic statistical procedures to indicate which Thoroughbreds are greater than others?

The relevant and parsimonious use of statistics is intended to assure racing fans that a truly critical, unbiased and fair appraisal of Thoroughbred performance can only be achieved through at least a basic analysis of the numbers representing how the horse ran a given race at a given place on a given day -- with all its interacting limitations of weather, jockey ability, equine condition and class.

No claim is made that statistical analyses are without limitations. However, they are as far superior to purely emotional statements about greatness as was Man o' War to the hopelessly outclassed Hoodwink in their 1920 Lawrence Realization race, or as was Secretariat to the entire Belmont field in 1973!

It is hoped that the reader will discern, as he or she progresses through this text, that fairness at every step has been the author's primary goal influencing the data comparisons between these splendid champions, whatever the final outcome.

I believe this will be abundantly clear to those not already driven by their own personal, unvoiced agendas.

CHAPTER 2

Notwithstanding Solomon, in a race speed must win.
-- Benjamin Disraeli

DRFC Data

It should be obvious that accurate and complete data are essential to any meaningful statistical analysis.

Beginning with the very basics, the word "datum" is singular and implies one measurement, sample, or value, normally numeric. The word "data" is plural and implies two or more measurements, samples or values.

All data for the analyses in this book were obtained from the 2000 publication issued by The Daily Racing Form, the DRFC (2).

For the remainder of this book and for convenience, the Champions reference, containing the complete past performance lines of 487 top champion Thoroughbreds, beginning with the 1890s and ending with the late 1990s, will be referred to as the DRFC.

Other commonly used terms or expressions will be abbreviated throughout after their first use, for more efficient reading. A list of abbreviations precedes the References section.

CB

The DRFC lists twenty data items directly race related on each of its performance lines. These items, reading from left to right in the text include:

1. Date of race
2. Name of race
3. Track abbreviation
4. Track condition
5. Distance
6. Surface (dirt or turf)
7. Fractional and finish times
8. Age and sex restrictions
9. Class of race and purse
10. Post position
11. Fractional calls with margins
12. Finish with margins
13. Jockey's name
14. Weight carried (jockey plus tack)
15. Equipment (blinkers, shadow roll, etc.)
16. Odds to $1.00
17. Speed Rating and Track Variant
18. First three finishers, weight carried and margins
19. Comment line
20. Number of starters

Other related items given in separate headers are:
1. Color, sex, year of birth, sire, sire's dam, dam's sire
2. Owner, Breeder, state where bred

This book uses a related sequence of three statistical methods – data sort, Linear Trend Analysis (LTA) and Limit or Three-Sigma Analysis (LA or TSA) – to determine which of 44 selected BHI horses and six specially recommended horses had the best overall racing record.

Points were assigned to each horse, depending on how their records compared, using each of these analysis techniques. Sort points *were not used* in the final rating. They were used to narrow the field of contenders for final analyses, based on LTA and LA.

Each data comparison method differs from the others, and the three combined techniques constitute a kind of data sieve that separates horses by ability.

When this three-layered process is completed, the horse having the highest score is considered a candidate for greatest horse. More than one horse may be so considered.

Each element of the sieve is explained as the data analysis process unfolds. Those having little or no statistics background need not worry. The book is mainly narrative. All statistics are explained as they are used.

Hopefully this unique study of equine greatness will prove unbiased, interesting and revelatory!

About the Selected Horses

Data Sorts: Before the data analyses proper (LTA and LA) were begun, the data for all horses were sorted into fourteen categories. The categories were taken either directly from the DRFC performance-line data or they were extensions (derivatives) of that data.

These fourteen sort criteria were each applied to both the two- and three-year-olds' performance data, and points were assigned each horse for each category based on how high in the total sort the given horse ranked.

The sort categories are fully explained in the next chapter. In some cases scant explanation is required because the category title explains itself. Fourteen categories were judged sufficient to allow each horse's particular strengths to be demonstrated. Beyond that, there is nothing magical about the number of categories assigned.

The remaining fifty-six of the top-100 BHI horses were not chosen because such was deemed unproductive.

Nine of the horses picked from the BHI list were rated below the top thirty-five, ranging to Lady's Secret, number seventy-six. Thus, an excellent overall sample was chosen.

Busher, Gallorette, Personal Ensign and Lady's Secret ranked 40, 45, 48 and 76, respectively. They were selected primarily to round out filly competition for Ruffian. Their data were important to supplement and contrast with hers. Ruffian ranked 35 in the top 100.

Sir Barton and Omaha, ranked 49 and 61, respectively, were chosen primarily because they won the Triple Crown and were thus judged deserving of selection for that reason alone. Noor, number 69, was selected due to his exemplary 5YO season.

Therefore, only Omaha, Noor and Lady's Secret, ranks 61, 69 and 76, were not ranked within the top 50 horses – except for the specially selected horses. The latter were not ranked in the top 100 Thoroughbreds of the twentieth century by BHI. They were recommended by Mr. Richard Sowers because of their outstanding performance records. (7)

In alphabetical order they were: First Flight, Gun Bow, Kincsem, Landaluce, La Prevoyante and Optimistic Gal. All but Gun Bow were fillies.

The General Sort Procedure

The selected horses were compared and ranked by performing two separate data sorts. Microsoft Excel® was the application used for all data analyses cited herein, except for Lumenaut's ® (designed to run with Excel) Shapiro-Wilk application which tests for normalcy of a distribution.

The first group of sorts was on the complete set of 2YO data. These data totaled over 360 records, an average of more than eight performance lines per BHI horse.

The records of each horse were sorted fourteen separate times, either low-to-high or vice versa, as appropriate for the particular performance measure, once for each category.

The sort results determined the top twenty (2YO) horses (plus ties) for each measurement. See Excursus B.

A second fourteen sorts was done, using the same categories and ranking system, for the three-year-olds' (3YO) data. These data contained over 500 records. See Excursus C.

Excursus B
Results of Data Sort for Top 20 Two-Year-Olds

Horse	Total Sort Points	BHI Rank
Seattle Slew	481	9
Ruffian - f	451	35
Spectacular Bid	436	10
Nashua	434	24
Colin	429	15
Count Fleet	429	5
Native Dancer	425	7
First Flight - f	423	None
Landaluce - f	420	None
Citation	411	3
Optimistic Gal - f	408	None
Dr. Fager	403	6
Equipoise	400	21
Damascus	396	16
Buckpasser	393	14
Personal Ensign - f	391	48
Alydar	390	27
Secretariat	387	2
Affirmed	381	12
Sunday Silence	378	31
La Prevoyante - f	373	None

Fillies Separated

Filly	Total Sort Points	BHI Rank
Ruffian	451	35
First Flight	423	None
Landaluce	420	None
Optimistic Gal	408	None
Personal Ensign	391	48

Excursus B – continued

La Prevoyante	373	None
Busher*	361	40
Gallorette*	253	45

*Below top 20 in 2YO overall sort

Excursus C
Results of Data Sort for Top 20 Three-Year-Olds

Horse	Total Sort Points	BHI Rank
Secretariat	479	2
Kelso	473	4
Damascus	454	16
Busher - f	443	40
Dr. Fager	443	6
Easy Goer	431	34
Seattle Slew	431	9
Man o' War	428	1
Alydar	422	27
Skip Away	421	32
Spectacular Bid	420	10
Sunday Silence	419	31
Native Dancer	414	7
Count Fleet	410	5
Citation	405	3
Swaps	401	20
Buckpasser	400	14
Round Table	398	17
Bold Ruler	397	19
War Admiral	395	13
Colin	393	15
Personal Ensign - f	378	48
Ruffian - f	378	35

Excursus C – continued

Fillies Separated

Filly	Total Sort Points	BHI Rank
Busher	443	40
Personal Ensign	378	48
Ruffian	378	35
La Prevoyante*	348	None
Gallorette*	287	45
First Flight*	279	None
Optimistic Gal*	273	None
**		

* Below Final Cut
** Intentionally blank in honor of the great Landaluce who did not live to race at age three.

The highest ranked horse in each category received forty-four points (the total number of BHI horses compared), while the last-ranked horse received one point. This scoring system allowed a possible 616 points for scoring highest in all categories. No horse accomplished that.

The highest scores were 481 and 479 points for the highest 2YOs and 3YOs, respectively. This testifies to the level of competition.

Since six of the forty-four BHI horses only raced until age three, and two of these (Forego and Cigar) did not race as two-year-olds, the data for ages four and five for the remaining horses was not included in the main study but was used in a modified study as will be explained later.

Thus, no matter how much the fans of any given horse that raced only at ages two and three would like to say he/she was the greatest of all time, there simply is no supporting data to compare him/her with other great horses at ages above three. Therefore, such claims are meaningless.

Similarly, horses like Cigar and Forego cannot be compared with Man o' War or Secretariat at age two, not because horses of different eras cannot be compared, as some claim, but because neither Cigar nor Forego raced at age two! It is impossible to say that either was greater because there is no factual evidence to support such statements.

This book and its conclusions, therefore, will disappoint some. It may even enrage others, considering the comments that enliven the Internet.

However, one can only use the data available, and these data limit the comparisons that may properly be made.

In this respect, the title of the BHI publication is misleading. Its rankings imply more than some horses actually produced.

Since Man o' War and Secretariat, as the two top-rated horses, did not race beyond age three, how can one say categorically that they were the number one and number two horses of the century? The century includes other ages.

One might say they were the top horses *for the ages at which they raced*, but no more than that may be accurately stated. Could either, for instance, have beaten Dr. Fager consistently as four-year-olds? Perhaps, but that is pure speculation – and they would have had to go some!

Could either, for example, have matched his one-mile run at Arlington Park that muggy Wednesday of August 28, 1968 when he shouldered 134 lb and set the still-standing world record of 1:32.20 s, equaled only by Najran carrying just 113 lb in 2003? (8) One can only guess.

Considering the above, we now specifically define and discuss the fourteen categories used in the two preliminary sorts. This discussion will clarify the basis of this study so that doubts or confusion concerning its objectives do not arise.

The crucial point to remember is that the data sorts themselves cannot and do not determine the greatest horse on any age or gender level.

The sorts act only as *initial selection tools* to narrow the field of final contenders. They also help determine whether they are self-consistent as selection tools in terms of the rankings made by the seven-member BHI panel.

If the sort results did not reasonably include at least some horses near the top of the BHI ranking, then they could be considered suspect or based on erroneous assumptions.

After all, the BHI voting panel was comprised of racing experts with vast experience. One would not suppose them to totally misjudge the merits of a select group of Thoroughbreds.

However, if the sort results are reasonably consistent with the BHI selection, good reason exists to assure us a valid sorting plan was used and that important and relevant data comparisons were made.

Chapter 3 explains each of the sort categories and also two specialized concepts from elementary physics. Don't let the word "physics" intimidate you.

Each concept is basic and is completely explained. These concepts are necessary parts of this study and are essential to consider, especially for those relatively new to Thoroughbred racing and the specialized way it is analyzed herein.

CHAPTER 3

Time must never be thought of as pre-existing in any sense;
it is a manufactured quantity
-- Hermann Bondi

Fourteen Sort Categories – Four Important Concepts

Sort Category 1: Average Distance Run

Average distance run was the first sort category and is now discussed formally for general reader clarification.

The *furlong* (abbreviation, f) is the basic, elemental unit of distance used in Thoroughbred racing. It is said to derive from an Old English word *furlang* meaning furrow long and referring to plowed fields.(5)

A furlong is one-eighth of a statute mile. Since the statute mile is 5,280.00 feet (hereafter abbreviated ft; mile, abbreviated mi), the furlong is 1/8 mi x 5,280 ft/mi, or 660.00 ft.

A good visualization of the furlong is obtained by imagining you are standing on one goal line of an American football field. If you walked to the opposite goal line, turned and then returned to your starting point, then turned and walked another twenty yards back toward the second goal line, you would have walked 660 ft or 1 f.

This book uses decimal notation for miles and feet for easier conversion of distances in furlongs or miles to feet, especially since average speed in feet per second (ft/s) is calculated from distance and time. Using decimal notation makes all calculations much faster and efficient.

Common short race distances for Thoroughbreds range from 2 f to 7 f. The races run at these distances are called *sprints*. All races longer than sprints, beginning at 1 mi, are called *route* races.

It does not take long to become accustomed to the furlong unit and to relate it both to fractional-mile and decimal-mile units.

For example, 7 f is seven-eights (7/8) of a mile. In decimal notation it is 0.875 mi, and in feet it is 7/8 mi x 5,280 ft/mi, or 4,620 ft.

Again, a 9 f race is 9/8 mi. In decimal notation this is 1.125 mi, and in feet it is 9/8 mi x 5,280 ft/mi, or 5,940 ft.

Sort Category 2: Average Speed

Speed is highly important as a datum in Thoroughbred racing. It is used as one of the fourteen sort factors in this study. Average speed is defined as the distance an object (horse in this case) travels divided by the time taken to travel that distance.

In this book, average speed(s) in ft/s are always used. They are derived from the relationship just stated: total *distance* (d) run divided by *time* (t) taken.

In equation form the verbal definition then becomes $s = d \div t$. Many often use *rate* or *velocity* to mean speed. That is fine, except one must remember that in physics the term *velocity* has the more specialized (vector) interpretation of *speed in a specified direction*.

For example, in 1973 Secretariat ran the fastest Kentucky Derby ever - a record still standing. His time was 1:59.40 s. This, for those new to the time notation of Thoroughbred racing, means one minute, fifty-nine and four-tenths seconds. It is also often called "one-fifty-nine and change" in racing lingo.

The DRFC always gives times as ending in fifths of a second - superscripted to the minutes and whole seconds - like this: $1:59^2$. This is identical to the 1:59.40 s stated above.

Be careful about those fifths of seconds! Remember that one-fifth of a second is 0.20 in decimal notation. Therefore, the two-fifths second of the above example translates into 0.40 seconds in decimal notation.

This means that Secretariat's average speed for the entire Kentucky Derby was 1.25 mi divided by 119.40 s. You can now see that using straight decimal seconds instead of the minute-second-fifths-of-second format is the only logical way to obtain quick average speed calculations!

Secretariat's average speed was, therefore, (1.25 mi x 5,280 ft/mi) ÷ 119.40 s. This equals (6,600 ft) ÷ 119.4 s = 55.28 ft/s, rounding to two decimal places as this book generally does throughout.

As you become familiar with the data presented herein, you will quickly recognize that average speeds over 55 ft/s for the longer route races are exceptional and indicate an outstanding Thoroughbred.

To give a more concrete feeling for these speeds, the faster Thoroughbreds can run extended distances at nearly the speed that would carry them from the pitcher's mound to home plate on a standard baseball diamond (60 ft-6 in) in 1.09 s, at Secretariat's Derby pace.

Concept 1: Kinetic Energy

Kinetic energy, and its related measure, *momentum*, are concepts taken directly from elementary physics. They are straightforward to understand, but this discussion may represent their first use in clarifying an extremely important problem in Thoroughbred racing – the *plate-weight issue*.

Many people say, for instance, that weight is extremely important regarding its affect on a given horse's performance. The kinetic energy formula applies numbers to this affect and indicates whether weight really plays as significant a role as claimed. Even so-called experts disagree on this point.

Kinetic Energy Discussion

To begin, every moving object, by definition, has an energy associated with it. Without going into the actual derivation and reasoning behind the validity of the kinetic energy concept, let it suffice to assure you that when a moving object's mass (m) is multiplied by one-half the square of its velocity or speed ($1/2v^2$), a meaningful number or quantity emerges which tells useful things about that object. That quantity is kinetic energy.

In algebraic language, kinetic energy (KE) equals $1/2 \cdot m \cdot v^2$, where m is the moving object's mass and v is its velocity or speed. The dots ($\cdot$) between 1/2, m and v^2 simply mean that the numerical values associated with these three symbols are multiplied together.

The mass of an object (m) is simply its weight (w), as measured by a common scale, divided by the acceleration due to earth's gravity (g) at the place where the weight is measured. That is, $m = w \div g$.

Since the acceleration due to gravity at mean sea level on earth averages 32.2 feet per second per second, commonly rounded down and shown as 32 ft/s^2, then an object's mass (without units) is just its weight divided by 32, or $m = w \div 32$.

The units for mass, in the British System of weights and measures, are lb·s^2/ft, since the unit for weight is the pound (lb) and the unit for g is ft/s^2.

Therefore, an object weighing 192 lb has a mass of: (192 lb) $\div$ (32 ft/s^2), or 6.0 lb·s^2/ft.

Readers unfamiliar with manipulating units in this way need not worry because they (the units, naturally) can be dropped, so long as one remains consistent. The *numerical value of the result* is what's really important, and that value's calculation can be simplified further by introducing a quantity directly related to, but simpler to calculate than, kinetic energy.

That quantity is called *momentum*. Its average is used as one of the data sort categories, but it is first introduced as reader background information.

Concept 2: Momentum

Momentum is symbolized by "p" in physics. The historic reason for using p is not completely known, but it is thought to be related to the Latin word "petere," meaning "to go for," according to Internet source Wikipedia. (9)

Momentum, by definition, equals a moving object's mass multiplied by its velocity, $p = m \cdot v$. It's that simple.

A helpful idea is to recognize that the expression for momentum is contained within the expression for kinetic energy. We can show this by manipulating the above formula for KE. It means that the two quantities are intimately related.

Using $1/2 \cdot m \cdot v^2$ for KE, notice that v^2 equals $v \cdot v$ because, by definition, the square of any quantity is that quantity multiplied by itself.

Therefore, an equivalent expression for KE is $1/2 \cdot m \cdot v \cdot v$. As long as we don't drop or change the symbols in an algebraic expression, we can group them as needed for ease of reading and interpretation.

By grouping the m and the first (leftmost) v inside parentheses, we have $1/2 \cdot (m \cdot v) \cdot v$. The quantity inside the parentheses is defined as the *momentum*. Thus momentum is a component or factor, if you will, of kinetic energy.

Figure 3.1 explains kinetic energy and momentum better than words. A ball having mass m and velocity v is shown moving to the right along a smooth surface, S. The expressions for momentum and kinetic energy are beneath the figure.

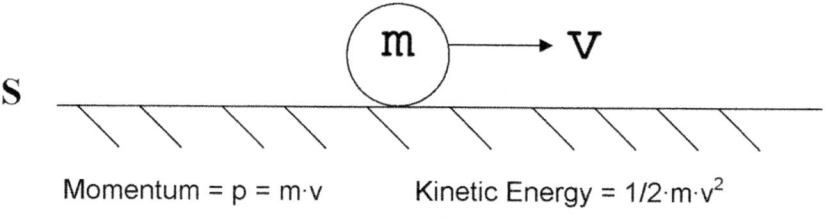

Momentum = $p = m \cdot v$ Kinetic Energy = $1/2 \cdot m \cdot v^2$

Figure 3.1
Formulas for calculating momentum and kinetic energy

Many horsemen say that speed isn't everything, and they're right in one sense. However, they usually don't qualify the comment by suggesting that kinetic energy and momentum **are** everything! These two quantities really are the best performance measures.

That is, the expressions for kinetic energy and momentum provide two useful and interrelated forms (the only scientific forms) for calculating the total energy of motion that a given horse generates during a race *by carrying the jockey, tack and racing plates around the track at a given average speed.*

It is questionable how many professional racing aficionados have considered this concept, but it is highly significant, as will be explained.

By using these basic and well-known physics concepts we can, for example, predict the maximum effect of steel versus aluminum racing plates on a given performance.

We can also obtain a precise indication of how much each pound extra a horse carries affects performance at a given distance. Such calculations can help resolve long-standing debates by placing upper limits on the effect.

Figure 3.2 is a graphic comparison of the two related quantities, momentum and kinetic energy.

Figure 3.2
Comparison Graph of Kinetic Energy and Momentum

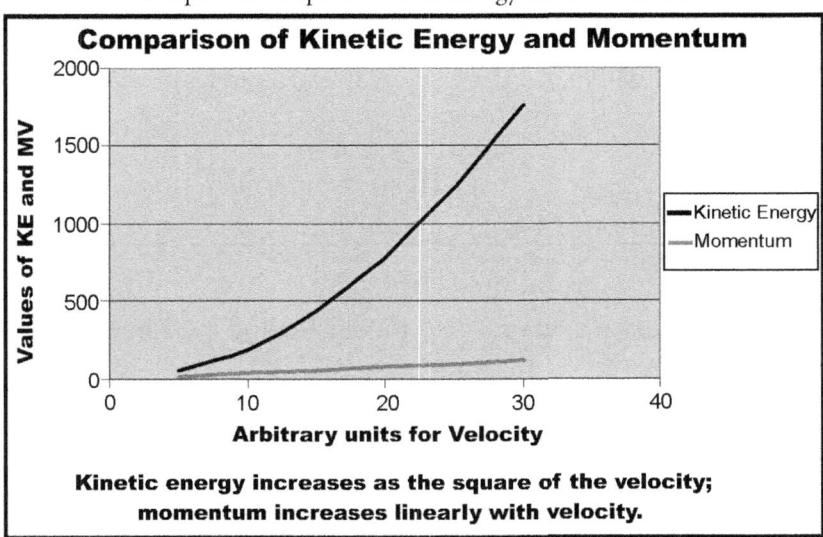

The Power of Using Kinetic Energy

An example using kinetic energy will clearly show the importance of this quantity for Thoroughbred racing.

Suppose Horse A runs 1.25 mi in the respectable time of 2:01.00 s (121.00 s) carrying 126 lb. If we assume that Horse A expended the *maximum* energy of which he was capable on that particular day and under those particular conditions, how long would it have taken him to complete the race carrying 127 lb?

First, calculate his average speed for the race when carrying 126 lb, and note that, for racing purposes and calculations, speed and velocity *are equivalent*. They are slightly different in physics, where *velocity is* defined as *speed in a definite direction*, but that does not change their numerical value.

Since a horse is nearly constantly changing directions throughout a race, velocity is not the appropriate quantity to use in such settings. Speed is the only logical choice.

Therefore, dividing 1.25 mi by the total time gives the average speed. For this example it is (1.25 mi x 5,280 ft/mi) ÷ 121 s = 6,600 ft ÷ 121 s = 54.54 ft/s, rounded to two decimal places.

Now, using $KE = 1/2 \cdot m \cdot v^2$, multiply the total mass carried (weight divided by 32) by Horse A at this average speed by 1/2 the average speed squared to find the kinetic energy: $(1/2 \cdot 126/32) \cdot (54.54)^2 = 5856.27$ **kinetic-energy units**, or 5856.27 KEU for simplicity.

As stated previously, we don't worry about units if we always express mass in the units (lb) ÷ (32 ft/s^2) and v (speed) in ft/s, because the numerical result is what's important and the units take care of themselves.

Therefore, we've determined that Horse A, carrying 126 lb and running 1.25 mi in 121 s generated a kinetic energy of 5856.27 units. How does this help us determine how fast he would have run the same race carrying 127 lb?

The answer is simple and at first seems trivial – but it's also scientifically correct! It involves no guessing or esoteric lore of the track.

We *assume* that the horse would have generated the same maximum number of KEU carrying 127 lb and put that number for weight into the equation for kinetic energy as follows: $1/2 \cdot (127/32) \cdot v^2 = 5856.27$ (use the same KE generated while carrying the lower weight).

Since we just assumed that Horse A expended all the kinetic energy *of which he was capable* while carrying 126 lb, we must assume that his kinetic energy carrying 127 lb in *the same race* would be identical.

There is no reason to assume otherwise, since this is a theoretical calculation used to find an upper boundary on how added weight affects speed and, therefore, time.

Now solve the above equation for the new value of v by multiplying both sides by the reciprocal of 1/2·(127/32), that is, 2·(32/127); [the reciprocal of 3/4, for example, is just the fraction flipped over, or 4/3] then take the positive square root of v^2 and you'll have the new speed, v = √(5856.27·2·32)/127 = √2951.19 = 54.32 ft/s, rounded to two decimal places.

For those rusty on square roots, taking the positive square root of a number merely involves finding the number that when multiplied by itself yields the given number. Modern calculators give the answer with one key press. For example, the square root of 9, symbolized √9, is ±3 because 3 x 3 = 9. You need not worry now about negative roots.

How will this new value for v affect the final time for the race? Divide 1.25 mi by the new calculated speed, 54.32 ft/s, and you find: 6,600 ft ÷ 54.32 ft/s = 121.50 s, rounding again to two decimal places.

Therefore, Horse A's time *will theoretically increase* from 121.00 s to 121.50 s for 1.25 mi **due to adding an extra one-pound impost!**

Used this way, the KE formula may seem magical, but it isn't. The question now is whether this accepted physics calculation fits with established racing wisdom?

In his book *Ainslie's Complete Guide to Thoroughbred Racing*, Tom Ainslie offers a list on page 266 which summarizes some time-honored numbers regarding the affect of added weight on racing time (10).

Relevant to the above example, his table indicates that adding one pound in a 1.25-mi race increases the running time by 1/5 s, or 0.20 s.

The value just derived is 0.30 s greater than Ainslie's. It is highly likely that the "real" value lies somewhere between the two, but it should be a revelation to racing enthusiasts to know that the <u>maximum</u> affect, based upon actual physics principles, *is at most 0.50 s.*

This result will be discussed further when a detailed comparison of the affect of steel versus aluminum racing plates on performance is given in Chapter 9.

Using the kinetic energy formula, we can dispel many misconceptions regarding how much steel racing plates hampered the performance of horses before 1946 when steel was used exclusively for making plates.

Sort Category 3: Average momentum per unit distance

We want unbiased sort categories, as far as possible. It is often difficult to achieve this.

The first of the derived sort categories is the average momentum divided by the average distance run by a given horse for all its races in one season.

By adding the momenta (singular – momentum) a given horse generated for each of its races, irrespective of distance run, and then dividing by the total distance run for all races, one should obtain an unbiased estimate of the momentum each horse generated per unit distance.

Obviously, some horses run faster at shorter distances than do others, and vice versa.

We desire sort categories that do not favor sprinters over "stayers," whenever possible. This category, then, attempts to provide that measure; it is a derived unit because it is not given per se in the DRFC raw data.

Momentum is simpler to calculate than is kinetic energy, and it is therefore used as one of the sort criteria for horses in both the juvenile and sophomore age brackets – especially because it also gives the horse credit for both average speed and weight carried, simultaneously. This is not generally done but should be.

For this study's data sorts, a simplified form of momentum was used. For racing calculation purposes, the total weight a horse carried, rather than the total mass of the jockey, tack and racing plates, was multiplied by the average speed to give the equivalent of momentum for each race.

Using weight instead of mass only changes the result by a factor of 1/32, since the acceleration due to gravity (technically 32.2 ft/s^2) is dropped from the m·v formula.

The numerical results are still proportional for all horses compared. They are simply a factor of 32 larger than they would have been had mass been used (m = w ÷ 32).

Using w·v instead of m·v gives numbers ranging from approximately the mid 5,000's to the mid 7,000's for every performance analyzed herein.

During Dr. Fager's exceptional world-record mile, cited in Chapter 2, he generated 7,718.42 momentum units, as defined above. This figure was the highest found throughout this study.

It cannot be over emphasized that units are unimportant if weight carried is consistently expressed in pounds and average speed is expressed in ft/s. All that is needed is a consistent comparison number between horses. Units, for racing purposes, are irrelevant.

In no case, based on DRFC data, did a championship-level horse win a race while generating a momentum less than 5,000 units. The reader will also see that momenta greater than 7,000 units are relatively sparse, and a number like Dr. Fager's, approaching 8,000, is rare.

There were just thirty-two such momenta out of 357 records (9%) for the two-year-olds and forty-nine of 511 (~10%) for the three-year-olds.

The minimum momenta for two- and three-year-olds were 5311.16 units and 5376.42 units, respectively.

To repeat, momentum assesses performance better than speed alone, because it includes the weight carried. It also provides a well-established scientific reference.

Sort Category 4: Δw·v/(Δ distance)

This number comprises another derived (not explicitly given in DRFC) sort category that was used for good reason. It represents the *change* in momentum (Δ is the capital Greek letter delta used in mathematics to denote change) that 2YOs experienced between

0.6875 mi and 0.75 mi. For 3YOs it measured momentum change between 1.00 and 1.125 mi.

These distances were used because most of the Thoroughbreds in this study ran at least one such distance at those respective ages.

Even top Thoroughbreds tend to slow down the farther they run. This point will be examined later when the linear trends are discussed.

Those horses slowing the least between these specified distances can certainly be judged to exhibit greater staying power or stamina, however one wants to express it.

Therefore, this category for sort purposes is seen as unbiased and one that will at least modestly indicate the superior horses from a stamina perspective. It therefore provides a reasonable way to reward those horses who showed less momentum change for a given distance range.

As always, anyone can argue the validity of using any sort criterion. However, they generally don't suggest a better method of comparison, and so for now the case rests.

All ratios for this category were taken to three decimal places to allow a finer and more discriminating sort.

Concept 3: Weight Carried

Weight carried by the horse was not used as a sort category per se, but it is important especially for calculating momentum.

The DRFC gives the weight of the jockey plus tack in its performance line listings. However, the racing plates a horse wears also have weight, although it is relatively small compared with the other weights.

In this study, steel plates were assigned an average weight of 1.8 lb for a complete set of four; aluminum plates were assigned an average weight of 0.78 lb per set. The assignment was not arbitrary.

The details of how these weights were determined are discussed later. They came from a farrier's Internet site. (11)

For momentum calculations, the total weight of jockey, tack and racing plates was used. In general, horses racing before 1946 only used steel plates. Horses after 1946 gradually transitioned to aluminum plates.

While it is difficult to determine the exact type of plate worn by a given horse – some current owners still use steel plates for better traction on some surfaces – the steel plate weights were included for pre-1950 races in order to be as fair and complete as reasonable regarding momentum calculations.

Sort Category 5: Number of Starters

Horses running in larger fields have some disadvantage versus horses racing in smaller fields. This is basically because they must maneuver more to find the most favorable running condition.

Although no definitive correlations have been published (the end of this chapter discusses correlations) for the affect of number of starters on final times, this study gives a slight point advantage to horses that consistently faced larger fields.

The correlations found in this study were 0.047 and -0.124, for all 2YOs and 3YOs, respectively.

The average number of starters was taken from the DRFC performance line data, and this number was used as a sort category.

Sort Category 6: Post Position

As for the case of starters, post position has a definite, though not easily calculated or consistent, effect on the final time of a given horse in a given race.

In this study it correlated 0.042 and -0.077 with final running times, for all 2YOs and 3YOs, respectively.

In many cases a position at or near the rail is favorable at the start of a race, but sometimes it isn't. This depends greatly on track drainage patterns, for one.

However, horses positioned at ten, twelve or more gates outside the rail are some forty to fifty feet from it and bear a distance disadvantage.

Their positioning means that they must first be maneuvered roughly along the hypotenuse of a right triangle extending from the center of their starting gate to a point nearer the rail before they and their jockey can begin sizing up the competition and establishing a running plan or race tactic.

Assuming a horse is forty feet outside the rail at the start and he runs along a line at 60-degrees with the gate array toward the rail, he will run eighty feet just to reach the point where the rail horse had only to run 69.28 ft to reach. Figure 3.3 illustrates this.

Figure 3.3
Extra Distance Run from Outside Post Position

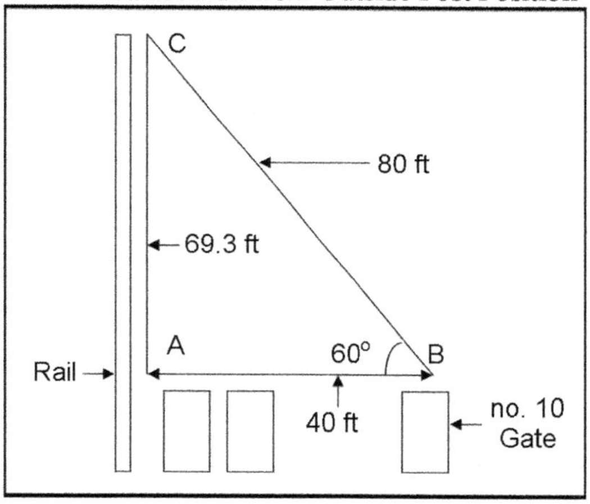

This extra distance is nearly 1.5 lengths, assuming a length is eight feet. It can significantly affect how the horse and jockey conduct the remainder of the race.

In this study average post position was used for a sort criterion, and the same proportion of points were given to horses who drew higher post positions from the rail as were to horses facing more starters, as explained in the previous sections.

Sort Category 7: Merit Figure

Each horse was assigned four points for winning, two points for placing and one point for showing. Zero points were given for finishing fourth or lower. This point scale was used for all races and for all horses, regardless of age.

The total points earned by each horse for a given year was divided by the total possible points he or she could have earned had all that year's races been won.

This percentage was called the *Merit Figure* and provided another sort criterion for this study. It rewards horses for percentage of wins but does not penalize horses who ran fewer races in one year than did others. It is therefore fair.

For example, if a horse won eight of ten starts and finished second in the two other starts, he earned thirty-six points.

The ratio of 36 to 40, i.e., 36/40, is 0.90. Multiplying by 100 then converts this into the Merit Figure of 90.00.

Concept 4: Standard Deviation – SD

The standard deviation (hereafter, SD), and its related variance, is certainly one of the most important concepts in statistics, as is the normal distribution. The SD is simply a type of average, but it is more involved than the common average, also called the mean.

The SD was not used as a sort category by itself, but it is presented now as a vital concept needed to understand both LTA and LA later in this text.

To calculate the SD, find the sum of the squared differences between the mean of the sample and each data measurement in the sample. Each of these differences is called a *deviation score*.

Then divide that result by n-1, the sample size minus 1, and take the square root. Every square root has two equal values, one plus and one minus, and these values together comprise the SD of the sample.

For example, the square root of 9 – symbol $\sqrt{9}$ – has two values, ± 3 (read plus or minus 3).

The negative standard deviation refers to values <u>below the mean</u>, and the positive standard deviation refers to values <u>above the mean</u>. Both values are equally important.

The standard deviation is important because many of the things we sample and measure follow a normal or near-normal distribution, as do most Thoroughbred running times for a given distance.

The standard deviation delimits exact percent values of where certain proportions of the area under the normal curve lie. This will be illustrated shortly when the normal curve is discussed.

For example, suppose a horse has run three races at 1.0 mi on fast tracks and has an average of 95 s and a standard deviation of 1.5 s.

If the times for these races were normally distributed, which can be checked using, for instance, the Shapiro-Wilk test, or S-W test, it can be confidently assumed that he would never run a given one-mile race on a fast track at *better or worse* than three standard deviations *below or above* his average. This is a significant insight!

NOTE: These limits are generally called the "3-sigma" limits in statistics jargon.

The above statement deserves the exclamation point. It means that the **fastest or slowest** times he would be expected to run one mile would be 95 s ± 3(1.5 s) = 90.5 s and 99.5 s, respectively. Thus, the three-sigma limits completely define his likely (at the 99.73% level) performance range!

From this fact and *no further data*, for example, we know that his chances of running a faster mile would be only 0.125 percent, due to the normal curve's properties.

Standard deviations will play a major role in the third and final part of this data comparison (Limits Analysis, or LA) to determine the candidate greatest horse.

The formula for calculating standard deviation is explained in Excursus D now. It is not essential that you know how to calculate a standard deviation, but you should convince yourself that you understand the procedure.

The *variance* is simply the square of the standard deviation (SD^2) and is used especially in the F-test, described later. Variance, being a number squared, is always positive.

Excursus D
Example Calculation of Standard Deviation Using
Seabiscuit's 1936 Data

In 1936 Seabiscuit, age 3, ran eight races at 8.5 f, or 1.0625 mi. He ran these races carrying from 110 to 116 lb.

His times (in seconds) were: 116.82, 104.22, 104.40, 106.57, 104.03, 105.94, 104.20, and 105.17.

Five steps are necessary to calculate the Standard Deviation (SD) for these times. The steps are first stated below and then are presented in tabular format for contrast.

1. Find the average of the data values – the eight times in this case.
2. Find the deviation scores for these times by subtracting their average from each of the individual times, X_i.
3. Square each of the deviation scores.
4. Add the squared deviation scores and divide by n – 1, the number of values minus one.
5. Take the square root of the answer from step 4. This is the standard deviation of the eight time values.

Each of the steps necessary to calculate the standard deviation of a set of data (eight time values in this case) is shown in the accompanying table below.

It is noteworthy that the first data entry, X_1, varies considerably from the other seven entries. This was because Seabiscuit ran that particular time on a muddy track. The remaining races represented by this data sample were run on fast tracks.

In fact, if X_1 is eliminated and a standard deviation calculated on only the remaining seven times, the new value is 0.991. This makes the difference between normal and non-normal Shapiro-Wilk tests for this set of times at the given distance (p = 0.179 vice p = 0.0001)! The test really is that sensitive!!

This difference also makes a dramatic change in calculating the likely limits of how fast Seabiscuit would run a given race of this distance.

For the higher SD value, his plus-or-minus three sigma limits are between 93.52 and 119.32 seconds. For the second SD value, these limits are between 101.96 and 107.91 seconds. You can see that the range is reduced by about 20 seconds.

Table for Excursus D
Seabiscuit's standard deviation calculations

Distance (miles)	Times in seconds (X_i)	Deviation Scores $(X_i - x)$	Squared Deviations $(X_i - x)^2$	Final Results
1.0625	$X_1 = 116.82$	10.40	108.19	Mean Squared
1.0625	$X_2 = 104.22$	-2.20	4.83	Deviation =
1.0625	$X_3 = 104.40$	-2.02	4.08	$129.54/n - 1 =$
1.0625	$X_4 = 106.57$	0.15	0.02	$129.54/7 =$
1.0625	$X_5 = 104.03$	-2.39	5.71	18.51
1.0625	$X_6 = 105.94$	-0.48	0.23	
1.0625	$X_7 = 104.20$	-2.22	4.92	Standard
1.0625	$X_8 = 105.17$	-1.25	1.56	Deviation Equals
	x = average = sum of $X_i/8 =$ 106.42		sum of $(X_i - x)^2 =$ 129.54	$\sqrt{18.51} =$ ± 4.30 Negative standard Deviations represent values below the mean, and vice versa for positive values.

Sort Category 8: Speed Rating – SR

Speed Rating and Track Variant are two data items published for each race by the DRFC.

The Speed Rating (SR) is determined by comparing a horse's final time for a given race to the fastest time in the *last three years* on the same track at the same distance and under approximately the same conditions.

For example, if a horse runs 3/5 s (0.60 s) faster than the fastest time of the previous three years winners, he earns a Speed Rating of 103. That is, he gets one point above 100 for each 1/5 s he broke the previous track record.

If he runs 3/5 s slower than the previous three years fastest time, he earns a Speed Rating of 97. Thus, one point has been subtracted from 100 for each 1/5 s by which he was slower than the fastest time.

Sort Category 9: SR divided by Group Speed Rating

The Group Speed Rating (GSR) is this author's modification of the DRFC's Track Variant. It is a term coined for this study, and it applies for a given day at a given track under the same stated conditions and distance.

It is computed by subtracting the DRFC's Track Variant value from 100. That's all! It then represents the *average of the speed ratings of all the winning horses for that day.* It now effectively becomes the Group's Speed Rating (GSR). It is considered a *derived quantity* for this study because Track Variants per se, as published by the DRFC, are calculated differently.

The ratio defined above is thus the Speed Rating (SR) of the winning horse divided by (100 – Track Variant), the GSR. In pure symbols this is written: SR ÷ GSR.

This ratio gives a direct and reasonably unbiased estimate of how a given horse's performance compares numerically with the average performances of other winners during the past three years – for the same track, rated condition and distance.

For example, if a horse attains a Speed Rating of 101 for a given track, distance and condition while the GSR for all other horses at the same track and distance for that day is 92, then his SR/GSR ratio is 101/92 = 1.098.

This automatically shows that the given horse ran better (i.e., greater than a 1.00 ratio) than the other horses for the same track and distance and under approximately the same conditions.

A caution about using this ratio is that the track records set many years ago were at slower times than currently and were perhaps more easily broken than are more recent records. Thus the SR/GSR ratio can be misleading. More will be said about this later in relation to foal crop size.

Sort Category 10: Time Between Races

The DRFC gives the date (month/day/year) of each race. By subtracting successive dates one can see how many days of rest (excluding workouts) a horse had between competitions.

If a horse runs all his races for a given year with only an average of ten days rest between, this is more impressive than a horse running all his races with an average of twenty days rest between and achieving identical results.

Horses with shorter rest periods should be rewarded, and the points assigned this factor does so in a relatively unbiased way.

Sort Category 11: Winning Margins (lengths won)

This sorting factor is simply the average number of lengths (also called margins) by which a horse won his races for a given year.

DRFC lists these *margins,* and they provide a readily available additional source by which to compare performances.

Sort Category 12: Number of Stakes Races Won

Stakes races are the most prestigious races, with the G-1, G-2 and G-3 races, in that order, being considered the most important. For example, the Triple Crown races are all G-1 stakes races. The stakes system of grading began in 1973.

This was an important sort criterion for both 2YOs and 3YOs. One point was given for each such race won, regardless of level.

Sort Category 13: Foal Crop

The foal crop is an oft-overlooked factor in judging the merits of a given horse.

Basically it is simply the total number of registered foals birthed by Thoroughbred mares during the same year as the given horse's birth.

Foal crop intimately though subtly determines the competition a given horse is likely to face during his prime racing years.

For instance, a horse born during a year when the foal crop is, say 10,000, generally faces less high-level competition at ages two and three, or even beyond, than does a horse born during a year when the foal crop was 40,000.

When one realizes that, as stated by Kent Hollingsworth in *The Kentucky Thoroughbred*, (12) only 2.5 percent of foals ever have a chance of winning a *single* stakes race in their careers, one sees the importance of this factor.

Table 2A lists the twenty horses that scored highest in either the two- or three-year-old sorts, or both, along with their foaling year, the corresponding foal crop size, and the number of possible single stakes champions that crop might yield based on the 2.5 percent factor.

Table 2A
Foal Crop Comparisons: Selected Top Sorted Horses

Horse (colts & fillies)	Year Foaled	Crop Size (thousands)	Likely Number of champions
Man o' War	1917	1.680	42
Equipoise	1928	4.503	113
War Admiral	1934	4.924	123
Count Fleet	1940	6.003	150
Citation	1945	5.819	145
Native Dancer	1950	9.095	227
Bold Ruler	1954	9.064	227
Kelso	1957	10.832	271
Buckpasser	1963	15.917	398
Damascus	1964	17.343	434
Dr. Fager	1964	17.343	434
Secretariat	1970	24.361	609

Table 2A – continued

Ruffian	1972	25.726	643
Seattle Slew	1974	27.586	690
Alydar	1975	28.271	707
Spectacular Bid	1976	28.809	720
Personal Ensign	1984	49.247	1231
Easy Goer	1986	51.296	1282
Cigar	1990	44.143	1104
Skip Away	1993	37.138	928

Sort Category 14: Records Set

The track records attained by the various Thoroughbred champions are marks of distinction separating them from their peers. As such, they are important sort factors.

As for the previous category, each horse was awarded one point for each race in which it achieved a SR of 100 or more. No extra weight was given to whether the record was a track, stakes, or even world record.

When the sorts for the 2YOs and 3YOs were completed, the results were as discussed in the next chapter.

There were, naturally, surprises. However, all in all, the sorts seemed reasonably supportive of the more qualitative ranking given by the BHI group of experts.

In that respect alone, the sorting process was worth its effort. Also, the fact that seven of the top ten BHI voted horses finished in the top twenty of the 2YO sort and that nine of the top ten finished in the top twenty of the 3YO sort lends at least some credibility to the sort categories.

However, the sort achieved more than credibility by narrowing the field of contenders whose records could more profitably be subjected to Linear Trend Analysis (LTA) and Limits Analysis (LA).

These latter two techniques then determined which horse was, by the only scientific judging criteria possible, a candidate for being greatest of all.

Correlation

A discussion of this important and often misunderstood statistical concept is necessary before proceeding.

Understanding correlation can help one dispel much misinformation regarding whether Thoroughbred data can be compared fairly from era to era, or even within eras with any level of confidence.

What, for instance, can or cannot be meaningfully said regarding a horse's running time in relation to various factors that might influence it?

The easiest way to show whether a relationship exists between two variables is by having the computer correlate them. The Microsoft Excel® application does this nicely.

Table 2B, a composite consisting of levels a, b, and c, gives correlations between running time and seven other parameters one might think would influence it significantly.

These three related tables show the correlations from data produced by Seabiscuit at ages two and three and by Dr. Fager at age three. These horses were selected primarily for their recognition and interest value and the fact that Seabiscuit ran more races than most of the top 100 BHI champions – twenty-two as a juvenile and fifteen as a sophomore. These are adequate, if not strictly large, sample sizes.

Statistical correlations range between -1.00 and +1.00. They can take any value between those limits. A minus correlation indicates that two variables are inversely related. That is, the larger one variable becomes, the smaller the second variable becomes, and vice versa.

Table 2B.a
Time Correlations for Seabiscuit: Age 2

Distance	Track	Condition	Weight
0.988	-0.098	-0.034	0.348
Post Position	Starters	Lengths Won	
0.175	-0.092	-0.364	

Table 2B.b
Time Correlations for Seabiscuit: Age 3

Distance	Track	Condition	Weight
0.806	0.250	0.433	0.166
Post Position	Starters	Lengths Won	
-0.058	-0.302	-0.111	

Table 2B.c
Time Correlations for Dr. Fager: Age 3

Distance	Track	Condition	Weight
0.998	0.591	-0.404	-0.323
Post Position	Starters	Lengths Won	
-0.632	-0.484	-0.589	

For positive correlations, both variables either decrease or increase concomitantly.

A perfect positive correlation is denoted by +1.00, while a perfect negative correlation is denoted by -1.00. Correlations near 0.00 indicate no relationship or a random relationship between variables.

Time versus Distance Run

Observe the *Time* variable in each of the Table 2B levels. Its correlations with the *Distance* variable are all positive, but they are not +1.00.

This may surprise you because we generally think that the longer distance a horse runs the longer time it takes, with no exception. Therefore, we might expect a perfect +1.00 correlation between time and distance run.

However, this is where reality takes over and tells us something different, if we take time (pun unintended) to listen.

First, it tells us that even the most presumed obvious relationships do not necessarily correlate perfectly in real life.

Second, if we think about this, we realize that simply because a horse may be running longer and longer races its time does not always increase smoothly with increasing distance.

It may be that for some of its shorter races a horse ran a slower time due to track condition, post position or interference by the field. All these affect its running time.

Therefore, it is actually unreasonable to expect a perfect correlation between any two variables due to all the influences a horse experiences during a race.

One additional correlation from Table 2.B will be discussed, simply to emphasize the points made above.

Time versus Weight Carried

Many people argue that weight carried (impost) must always be considered when comparing horses. That is, if two horses ran a series of races at the same distances, over tracks having identical conditions, and one horse carried several pounds more than the other, they would argue that the horse carrying the heavier weight was automatically disadvantaged and would have done better carrying lower weight.

This is not necessarily true, as indicated by Table 2.B.

The data for Seabiscuit at ages two and three show that his times correlated positively, although fairly low, with the weights he carried.

The positive correlation means that, in general, the heavier the impost Seabiscuit was assigned, the slower he ran (longer times taken).

The opposite apparently held for Dr. Fager at age three! His times show a negative correlation of -0.323 with weights carried. That is both interesting and instructive.

Although we cannot tell exactly what this means, it indicates that, at least on some occasions, Dr. Fager ran better (faster times) when he was assigned heavier weights!

Coefficient of Determination – COD

One additional piece of information is needed to better appreciate the implications of correlation. That is, one must square the correlation coefficients in Table 2.B to find what percent of change they tend to accompany in the *Time* variable.

The resulting value is given the academic sounding name, "Coefficient of Determination." Its abbreviation is COD for the remainder of this book. It is generally symbolized as R^2.

Note that the word "accompany" was selected with deliberation. Many people think that correlation implies causation. That is generally untrue. All it means is that two or more sets of numbers have a certain numerical relationship with each other. Causation *may* link the variables, but it would take additional evidence to show it.

Returning to correlation proper, if we square any number, positive or negative, the result is always positive. Squaring Dr. Fager's -0.323 time-weight correlation coefficient gives the COD 0.104. Multiplying that result by 100 converts it into the percent value 10.4.

This indicates that, for Dr. Fager's case only, increased weights carried help explain 10.4 percent of the change in running times. This suggests that higher imposts helped Dr. Fager run faster!

The above may not make immediate sense, but it's difficult to argue with the numbers. If you examine Dr. Fager's past performance record as a 3YO, you'll find that he raced nine times.

Three races were at 8 f, two were at 9 f, three were at 10 f; one was at 7f. In two of these races he ran faster times, at identical distances, carrying more weight. His imposts for all races ranged from 120 lb to 128 lb, a fairly narrow range.

This emphasizes that one cannot automatically say that a horse has been discriminated against by giving it a higher impost. Some horses, for reasons unknown, simply seem to run faster under reasonably heavier weights. Perhaps they actually sense and enjoy the challenge.

In fact, Dr. Fager still holds the world record for 8 f. It was tied once in 2003, as was mentioned earlier.

In August 1968 at Arlington Park he carried 134 lb and ran 8 f in a slightly incredible 92.20 s! Of all world records listed for dirt tracks through 2007, this is by far the heaviest impost carried by any horse establishing such a record. Najran, who tied Dr. Fager's record for the mile in 2003, carried only 113 lb.

For convenient future reference, remember that a correlation must be at least ± 0.707 to indicate a possible 50% interaction between two variables (COD = 0.707^2 = 0.50). Correlations this high or higher are relatively scarce in most areas of research and data analysis.

For example, IQ scores seldom correlate 0.707 or higher with any intellectual aptitude or educational variable against which they are compared. And yet most people continue to believe that IQ tests actually measure an important quality of the mind and define a person's capabilities! As the Gershwin's song says, "It ain't necessarily so!" (13)

When the linear trends of the champion Thoroughbreds are discussed later in the book, you will see that many of their correlations between distance run and time taken are above 0.990! This is nearly unheard of in research and is also extremely fortunate for supporting the validity of the comparison method – LTA – between horses made herein.

CHAPTER 4

The great thing about time is that it goes on.
-- Arthur S. Eddington

The Data Sort for Two-Year-Olds

The data sorts for the 2YOs and 3YOs yielded interesting and surprising results.

Of the fourteen sort criteria, six were taken directly from the data in the DRFC's past performance lines using only averages.

These criteria were: average post position, average number of starters, average time between races, average margins (lengths) by which races were won, average distance run and average speed.

The remaining criteria were based directly on data given by the DRFC, and they are therefore derivatives of DRFC data.

These criteria are: *average momentum per mile, change in momentum per unit distance, merit figure, speed rating, ratio of speed rating to group speed rating, number of stakes won, foal crop size and records held.*

To reemphasize, there is absolutely nothing contrived or manipulated about any of the derived sort criteria.

These criteria were not used in any manner to favor a given horse. Rather, they were used because it was felt they were good indicators of Thoroughbred performance and would thus help differentiate between quality levels. This was the intent in structuring them and using them for the study.

Note that, of the top ten horses chosen by the BHI panel, seven finished in the top twenty of the 2YO data sort. Similarly, nine of the top ten ranked BHI horses finished in the top twenty of the 3YO data sort.

Table 3 below lists the top 2YOs based on the sorted data. Biographies for Ruffian and Seattle Slew follow.

Table 3
Top Twenty Two-Year-Olds Based on Sort Criteria

Colts/Fillies	Sort Rank	BHI Rank	Total Points
Seattle Slew	1	9	481
Ruffian*	2	35	451
Spectacular Bid	3	10	436
Nashua	4	24	434
Count Fleet	5	5	429
Colin	5	15	429
Native Dancer	6	7	425
First Flight*	7	None	423
Landaluce*	8	None	420
Citation	9	3	411
Optimistic Gal*	10	None	408
Dr. Fager	11	6	403
Equipoise	12	21	400
Damascus	13	16	396
Buckpasser	14	14	393
Personal Ensign*	15	48	391
Alydar	16	27	390
Secretariat	17	2	387
Affirmed	18	12	381
Sunday Silence	19	31	378
La Prevoyante*	20	None	373

* Fillies indicated with asterisk. Fillies held places 2, 7, 8, 10, 15, and 20 of the top twenty positions.

Biography of Ruffian

Ruffian's 451 total sort points earned second place to Seattle Slew's 481 points within the fourteen basic sorting categories for 2YOs. It seems appropriate to present her biography and Seattle Slew's as an interim tribute before proceeding to the remaining data analyses for 2YOs.

Although "Slew" outscored Ruffian by thirty points for first place, he undoubtedly would not mind her going first, gentleman that he was!

Winning the sort *does not imply* that the other colts or fillies could not or did not outperform her in categories such as average speed, momentum or on other sort criteria. However, for some categories, it is nearly axiomatic in Thoroughbred racing that colts outperform fillies.

Nevertheless, she definitely outranked the other fillies included (alphabetically: Busher, First Flight, Gallorette, Landaluce, La Prevoyante, Optimistic Gal and Personal Ensign) in sort points.

Such issues regarding colts versus fillies will be examined later, but first a synopsis of Ruffian's career is given, as is fitting for her class and distinction. The same format followed herein will be repeated for the results of the 3YO sort.

Ↄ

The great Ruffian was a dark bay filly foaled on Monday April 17, 1972. She was by Reviewer (sired by Bold Ruler) out of Shenanigans by Native Dancer.

Except that the genetic odds for producing greatness remain strangely constant regardless of illustrious forebears, such distinguished grandsires would nearly lead one to expect the brilliance she displayed during her tragically brief career.

Ruffian was trained by Frank Whiteley for owner Stuart S. Janney, and her regular jockey, for all but two of her career starts, was Jacinto Vasquez.

Significantly, BHI referred to her as one of the truly great Thoroughbreds of the twentieth century. Their statement is certainly upheld by these preliminary sort results.

Ruffian's record for her juvenile year (1974) was an unblemished five-for-five. She earned her total 451 sort points by scoring points in all fourteen of the possible sort categories.

She averaged an impressive 32.2 points for the fourteen categories. Her lowest score was twelve points for the category *Number of Starters*. She scored a perfect forty-four points in both the *Merit Figure* and *Speed Rating* categories and forty-three points in the categories *Average Speed*, *Speed Rating/Group Speed Rating*, *Lengths Won* and *Records Held*.

Her fastest speeds were generated at Aqueduct, Saratoga and Belmont, respectively, at distances of 5.5 f and 6 f, the only distances she ran as a 2YO.

The derived category *Speed Rating divided by Group Speed Rating* (SR/GSR) indicates how a horse's performance compares to the *average performances* of all winners at the same track on the same day for the same distance and under as identical conditions as practicable.

Ruffian scored second in this category with forty-three points to Spectacular Bid's forty-four. Her SR/GSR was 1.136 while "The Bid's" was 1.148.

In the *Average Winning Margin (Lengths) Won* category Ruffian held second place by averaging 9.15 lengths per win to Landaluce's 9.3 lengths per win and first place.

The five performances each of these fillies produced in their juvenile season verge on the unbelievable.

This seems especially true for the shorter sprint distances of 5.5 f and 6 f for Ruffian, without taking any credit from Landaluce.

Ruffian's sprints led one turf writer, Steven Davidowitz (14), to speculate that she could have beaten Secretariat consistently at six furlongs. The correctness of this statement is shown later!

In contrast, the great West Coast runner, Landaluce, ran in five races at distances from 6 f to 8.5 f. Her winning margins, in chronological order for the year's races, were: 7, 21, 6.5, 10 and 2 lengths at the respective distances of 6 f, 6 f, 8 f, 7 f and 8.5 f.

By comparison, the next closest rival fillies in this category were Personal Ensign, La Prevoyante and Optimistic Gal. They averaged 6.44, 5.73 and 4.96 lengths per win, respectively.

To highlight the competition in this category, although one must caution comparing the colts with the fillies, the great Seattle Slew averaged 6.08 lengths per win, while the undisputedly great Secretariat averaged 3.28 lengths per win.

As mentioned earlier, *Foal Crop* is a highly important but generally overlooked category for statistical sort consideration, or any consideration of greatness, for that matter.

Ruffian's foal crop for 1972 is officially registered as 25,756 (15). That crop size earned her ninth place and 36 sort points.

More will be said later about the fairness of assigning points for this category. However, readers may be assured that it is eminently reasonable considering that competition varies directly from year to year with the size of the crop into which a given foal is birthed.

At age two, Ruffian equaled two track records, one in her maiden race at Belmont, the other about three weeks later in the Fashion-G3 stakes race. These performances tied her for second place with four others and garnered forty-three sort points.

Ruffian won four stakes races at age two, and she earned 38 points in the *Stakes Won* sort category.

These points tied her for seventh place in the category with six colts: Alydar, Count Fleet, Nashua, Sysonby Tom Fool and Whirlaway.

In summary, for the fourteen total sort categories, Ruffian at age two was awarded 451 total points.

A closer analytic view of her performances is presented after the next chapter which gives a similar overview of the 3YO sort results.

Biography of Seattle Slew

Seattle Slew finished thirty points ahead of Ruffian in the 2YO sort and 94 points better than number-seventeen ranked Secretariat (BHI rank 2), obviously one of the great Thoroughbred colts of all time.

It must be cautioned, again, that the sort was used merely to narrow the field of final contenders to the "best of the best." By itself, it does not define the best of all.

Seattle Slew was a dark bay colt foaled on Friday February 15, 1974 and raised at White Horse Acres near Lexington, Kentucky. His sire was Bold Reasoning (grandson of Bold Ruler), and his dam was My Charmer. Both sire and dam were directly related to Nasrullah. Bold Ruler was a son, and My Charmer was a great granddaughter.

Seattle Slew was a special Thoroughbred. Although rated nine by BHI, he undoubtedly deserved a higher rank.

For one, he raced for three years, at ages 2, 3 and 4, winning an impressive fourteen of seventeen starts. He finished "off the board" just once. That was on July 3, 1977 (age 3) at the Swaps-G1 stakes at Hollywood Park where he was unexplainably fourth by sixteen lengths. His two "place" finishes were the only additional blemishes on his otherwise stellar record.

However, he remains the only horse to have won the Triple Crown while undefeated. His jockey, for the first thirteen of his seventeen races, was Jean Cruget. After a disagreement between Mr. Cruget and Slew's owners regarding appropriate training methods, Angel Cordero, Jr. guided Slew around the track for his last four races, losing by a nose just once.

Slew exceeded a speed variant of 100 twice. He had a 102 for a 7 f allowance race at Hialeah on the first outing of his sophomore year. He scored an impressive 109 for a 10 f race at Belmont, the Woodward-G1 stakes race, by finishing in two minutes flat while winning by four lengths.

After he retired from racing, Slew's first foal crop included a filly who, along with First Flight, is really the only one to seriously rival Ruffian at two years of age in this study, Landaluce.

One of Seattle Slew's sons, Swale, won the 1984 Kentucky Derby by 3.25 lengths and the Belmont Stakes by four lengths but finished seventh by 6.75 lengths in the Preakness. Had he won, Seattle Slew and Swale would be only the second father-son tandem (Gallant Fox and Omaha being first) to have achieved that feat. Swale's performance line for the Preakness merely states "bothered."

Seattle Slew averaged 34.4 points per sort category. His lowest placement was in the Δ *momentum* category, in which he was in forty-first place with four points. He scored forty or more points, however, in *average distance run, momentum at 0.75 miles, merit figure, lengths won and records* categories.

The following chapter discusses the sort results for the 3YOs.

CHAPTER 5

Time is just one damn thing after another.
-- Anonymous

The Data Sort for Three-Year-Olds

Table 4 lists the top twenty (with ties) 3YOs based on the sorted data. The top twenty 3YO sort horses advanced to Linear Trend Analysis (LTA), just as did the top twenty 2YOs. In keeping with the 2YO presentation format, a brief biography for the top two horses in the 3YO sort follows the sort results.

We then proceed to LTA for the 2YOs and 3YOs. Finally, Limits Analysis (LA) is applied to the top ten horses (plus ties, if any) from the LTA capped by the candidate greatest horse(s) selection.

CB

Secretariat and Kelso finished number one and two in the 3YO data sort.

Table 4

Top 20 (and ties) Three-Year-Olds Based on Sort Criteria

Horse	Sort Rank	BHI Rank	Total Points
Secretariat	1	2	479
Kelso	2	4	473
Damascus	3	16	454

Table 4 – continued

Busher*	4	40	443
Dr. Fager	4 (tie)	6	443
Easy Goer	5	34	431
Seattle Slew	5 (tie)	9	431
Man o' War	6	1	428
Alydar	7	27	422
Skip Away	8	32	421
Spectacular Bid	9	10	420
Sunday Silence	10	31	419
Native Dancer	11	7	414
Count Fleet	12	5	410
Citation	13	3	405
Swaps	14	20	401
Buckpasser	15	14	400
Round Table	16	17	398
Bold Ruler	17	19	397
War Admiral	18	13	395
Colin	19	15	393
Personal Ensign*	20	48	378
Ruffian*	20 (tie)	35	378

*Filly

Biography of Secretariat

He has adoringly been christened everything from *Big Red* to *Super Horse* to *The Horse God Built*, by enthusiastic admirers, but no turn of prose seems quite elegant enough to frame the ability of this truly superb champion from Meadow Stable in the town of Doswell, Commonwealth of Virginia.

He was foaled at The Meadow on Monday March 30, 1970. He was the product of Bold Ruler, one of the great Thoroughbred sires of all time, and dam Something Royal.

Christopher T. Chenery owned the Meadow Stable, but he was in poor health and so his daughter, Helen (Penny) Chenery basically managed

Secretariat's career. Mr. Chenery passed away in January of 1973, sadly unable to appreciate the full glory that was to befall his burnished chestnut colt with the three white stockings, a star and a stripe.

To state bare fact and say that Secretariat was the first Thoroughbred to win the Triple Crown in the twenty-five years since Citation won it in 1948 misses the point entirely.

It was how he won it that encapsulates his true greatness.

Churchill Downs, 1973

Secretariat drew post position ten for the Kentucky Derby. From there, he basically ambled leisurely across the track as the gates flung wide, content to fall in behind the field.

Mrs. Chenery once said during a taped interview that he lagged behind horses early in races because he was "mugged" at Aqueduct in his maiden race on Tuesday July 4, 1972. That, incidentally, was the only race in which he finished as low as fourth. He was nearly knocked down, but he recovered and remained wiser because of the incident. He thereafter avoided early confrontations with other runners.

Not until about the clubhouse turn did Secretariat begin to move. Then, as though the extra distance was totally inconsequential, he simply ran around the field's right flank and began passing the other twelve horses so that he resembled "a *Rolls-Royce in a field of Volkswagens*," as Chick Lang, former Pimlico general manager engagingly phrased it.

To shorten a long story, he won the Derby by 2.5 lengths over the game Sham. However, his winning time – still the fastest recorded in Derby history after thirty-four years – of 1:59.40 s is misleading.

As is more fully discussed later, Secretariat essentially added about 105 ft to the stated length of the Derby by his racing tactic.

If you realize that he was at least fifteen feet from the rail around both quarter-mile turns and ran about eleven feet more from his number-ten post position to gain initial proper alignment with the field, you can easily calculate that his time for the stated Derby distance of 10 f was actually closer to 117.50 s.

Only Monarchos in 2001 has remotely approached Secretariat's official Derby time. Monarchos registered 1:59.88 s in that race.

Had Secretariat drawn the rail position, he likely would have been nearly two seconds faster than his official time! Needless to say, that is a record that probably would never be broken, especially when one reviews a sampling of the stellar Thoroughbreds who have won the Derby between 1973 and 1989 but did not better or even approach his time. It reads like a *Who's Who* of the sport.

Foolish Pleasure, Bold Forbes, Seattle Slew, Affirmed, Spectacular Bid, Genuine Risk (f), Swale, Spend A Buck, Ferdinand, Alysheba, Winning Colors (f) and Sunday Silence are just some of the great horses who fell short of Secretariat's time by anywhere from 0.80 s to 5.60 s.

Each of these champions ran on fast-rated tracks with the exception of Sunday Silence. The track was muddy for his race, and that undoubtedly accounts for much of the 5.60 s longer time of 2:05.00 s he ran relative to Secretariat. The two fillies carried 121 lb. But all these horses certainly had the same basic running conditions as did Secretariat, and so his performance cannot be derogated in any manner.

Old Hilltop – Pimlico, 1973

A similar story unfolded in the Preakness. Secretariat lagged the field at first; he began his move at about the clubhouse turn, passed the field on the outside, overtook the leader Sham, and scored another 2.5-length victory.

Secretariat's "official" time by the Pimlico timer was 1:54.40 s, but, as is well known, it chose that particular day and race on which to malfunction.

Two separate timers from the Daily Racing Form clocked Secretariat at a second faster – 1:53.40 s. An independent film comparison also verified his faster time. It showed that Secretariat would have beaten the 1971 record setter, Canõnero II by two lengths.

However, for whatever reasons, as of June 2007, the Maryland Racing Commission has declined to recognize Secretariat's faster time. (16)

All this is, however, academic. If one calculates the actual "trip" Secretariat took, as in the Derby, running well outside the rail around the turns, one sees that he actually ran at least 6370 ft – 100 ft more than the stated race distance of 6270 ft or 9.5 f.

His average speed was therefore 56.17 ft/s. Had he run the true 6270 ft at that pace, his time would have been 111.62 s!

That time would summarily have precluded the names of Tank's Prospect, Louis Quatorze and Curlin as current co-record holders of Preakness time. It would likely have set a standard never to be surpassed.

If further supporting argument for the above statements is needed, consider a track at Elmont, New York.

Belmont Park, 1973

Secretariat drew and held the rail position throughout the race, and he set a still-standing world record on dirt for the 12 f. His time was 2:24.00 s. As of 2004, no horse came closer than 2:26.00 s - Easy Goer in 1989, and A.P. Indy in 1992.

More pertinent to the argument, at 10 f into the race, the length of the Kentucky Derby, Secretariat's time was 119.00 s. He thus eclipsed his Derby record time for the same distance by 0.40 s. And yet Ron Turcotte, his jockey, later said he was moving easy!

A separate LTA calculated for the Belmont alone shows that Secretariat must have reached the 9.5 f point in 113.11 s – nearly 0.30 s faster than the current accepted Preakness record.

Post Triple Crown

Secretariat's overall racing record, although notable, was not as good as, for instance, Man o' War's. He finished 21-16-3-1 with the single fourth place finish in his maiden effort at Aqueduct.

There are valid reasons for most of his losses: the mugging in his maiden race at Aqueduct, a mouth abscess in the Wood Memorial, the rather dubious disqualification in the Champagne Stakes and a fever in the Whitney. Perhaps only in the Woodward would the sloppy track not be a truly valid excuse for losing.

Secretariat earned 479 of a possible 616 sort points in the 3YO category. He averaged 34.2 points per category.

His lowest point score was 20 (Time Between Races); his highest point totals were 42 (Speed Rating and Records Held).

Secretariat edged Kelso in the 3YO sort by just six points. One could easily argue they were equivalent at age three, based on this data. Kelso's biography is now presented to honor his distinction.

Biography of Kelso

Kelso's 473 sort points earned him second place, six points below Secretariat. It seems fitting that these champions, rated fourth and second, respectively, by the BHI panel, finish first and second in this data sort.

The sort, to reiterate, does not pick the candidate greatest horse. There is always the danger of slipping into that mode of thinking. The sort was designed to separate the best from the best so that the remaining analyses would be simpler. The sort is only intended to narrow the competitors for further analysis.

Nevertheless, by any logical standards, Secretariat and Kelso definitely deserve these high rankings, and it is gratifying that the sort design was consistent in selecting these preliminary candidates.

Kelso's 473 sort points of a possible 616 translate to an average of 33.8 points per category. In gaining these points, his lowest category was in momentum change between 1 mi and 1.125 mi (Δ *momentum*), for which he gained ten points. His highest category, *SR/GSR*, netted him forty-one points.

He earned forty points in three categories: *Speed Rating, Lengths Won* and *Records Held*.

Kelso was a dark bay gelding, foaled on Thursday April 4, 1957 at Claiborne Farm near Paris, Kentucky. His sire was Your Host, and his dam was Maid of Flight.

On the distaff side, he claimed none other than Count Fleet as a grandfather and Man o' War as a great grandfather. With forebears like that, one would expect greatness, however sporadically its genes may distribute within Thoroughbred blood.

Although not a Triple Crown winner, Kelso nonetheless had an outstanding career. He raced at ages two through nine, having sixty-three total starts.

Of these, he won thirty-nine, placed in twelve and showed twice. As simple arithmetic shows, this means he was "off the board" just ten times in his career. Of those ten times, he was fourth on five occasions. His worst finish – eighth place by 9.5 lengths – came in a 7 f race on a fast-rated track at Hollywood on May 23, 1964. Kelso carried 130 lb to the 124 lb borne by the winner, Cyrano. The comments on Kelso's performance line for that race state simply "Dull effort."

Undoubtedly Cyrano's greatest claim to fame was that he once beat Kelso!

Kelso's accomplishments far overshadow any failures he may have experienced. He won five Horse of the Year titles, was a divisional champion five times, set or equaled eight track records and also set three American standards.

Among Kelso's records are included: the fastest 13 f by a 3YO (2:40.80 s; 1960 Lawrence Realization Stakes); the fastest 16 f (3:19.20 s; 1964 Jockey Club Gold Cup); fastest 16 f by a 3YO (3:19.40 s; 1960 Jockey Club Gold Cup) and one of the ten fastest 12 f turf races (2:23.80 s; 1964 Washington, D.C. International). (3)

Kelso's primary jockey, for thirty-four of his total starts, was Ismael Valenzuela. Two notable riders, for four and fourteen of his starts, were Willie Shoemaker and Eddie Arcaro, respectively.

It was Arcaro who once remarked that Kelso could beat anything at any distance. This is not overstated.

Kelso died on Sunday October 16, 1983 at Mrs. Richard du Pont's Woodstock Farm in Maryland, aged twenty-six.

❦

This concludes the sort results for candidate best 3YO Thoroughbred of the twentieth century.

The following chapter gives a brief overview of the basic statistics needed to fully understand the final analyses – LTA and LA.

These statistics are then applied to the data of the twenty highest-scoring horses, plus ties, of the fourteen sort categories just summarized for both the 2YOs and 3YOs.

It is interesting that, of the twenty-three 3YOs, including ties, scoring highest in the sort and advancing to LTA, sixteen were ranked in the top twenty of the BHI listing.

This lends further consistency to both sets of rankings, if not absolute validity.

CHAPTER 6

You must remember this – a kiss is still a kiss, a sigh is just a sigh. The fundamental things apply as time goes by.
-- Herman Hupfeld

Winning a data sort, as described in the previous two chapters, is the first step toward being eligible for candidate greatest horse status. The twenty winning horses, plus ties, in both the 2YO and 3YO categories must now pass the more stringent tests of LTA and LA, where these latter abbreviations for Linear Trend Analysis and Limits Analysis will hereafter be used.

The critical reader may, in fact, have already objected to being given the impression that Seattle Slew was the greatest 2YO Thoroughbred of the twentieth century or that Secretariat was the greatest 3YO, as could be implied by the data sort. However, the sort was only used for screening.

Having reiterated this point several times, we proceed to the serious business of applying actual data analyses.

Sorts, like all data handling techniques, have limitations. For example, a sort may favor a single performance such as average speed or momentum or lengths won, as has already been explained. Simultaneously, they may make total overall performances appear less impressive than wins in certain categories such as *Speed Ratio*.

The data sort for 2YOs, in fact, ranked the undisputedly great Secretariat below Seattle Slew while also ranking Man o' War below the top twenty by fourteen points. Thus, a just accounting must now be made to determine whether the sort's conclusion withstands the harsher light of statistical analysis.

As has been aptly stated, "Once a number is produced, something, perhaps everything, of value has been lost. Like so many tabulations, the numbers disguise individual stories of heroism and betrayal, triumph and defeat, and force them into bleak summaries." (17)

A basic overview of key statistics is now warranted, especially for the reader new to the subject. It is also good to keep all readers focused on what this book is attempting to accomplish.

However, the overview will not be a "paralysis-by-analysis" exercise or a statistics primer.

Since many readers are totally unfamiliar with statistical concepts, and since basic statistics are needed for even an elementary analysis of racing data, then the following overview of the subject is mandatory if one is to reach beyond the realm of purely emotional convictions and speculations about a given horse's greatness.

Having said this, the minimum essentials of statistics are introduced. It is then shown how these essentials are used to extend and refine the sort results using LTA and LA.

Key Statistical Concepts

Ten basic concepts are required to appreciate the level of statistics used in the remainder of this study. Although complete statistical comparisons are ultimately based on computer analyses of algebraic-like equations, the reader will be spared most of the background mathematics.

The mathematics needed to grasp the essential purpose of statistics are actually no harder than eighth- or ninth-grade level – at least by the teaching standards of the time when the author was learning math basics.

After this survey of the ten basic statistics concepts and their usage, immediate application follows concerning how the truly greatest 2YO and 3YO Thoroughbreds of the twentieth century may be identified.

When you see how straightforward these statistical concepts are and how, when used properly, they illuminate questions regarding comparisons you may have thought unanswerable, you will view everyday events and their relation to statistics much differently.

Your attention to these concepts will be amply rewarded.

Concept 1: Populations and Samples

Nature gives us entire *populations*, but we can usually only handle *samples* for practical reasons. A sample is a portion of some population.

For instance, if you needed to know the average height of all *American males age twenty through forty-four*, you find there are slightly over fifty-one million of such individuals from which to sample, as of the 2000 census (18).

You obviously can't measure the heights of all these men (the actual *population*) due to practical considerations such as money, time and logistics, to name only three.

Therefore, you must select a *sample* — a smaller group within the population and representative of it.

Your sample will contain some reasonable number, perhaps thirty, more or less, of such males. It will give you sufficient data to make a good *estimate* of the average height — probably in inches to the nearest one-eighth inch being sufficient.

This would be acceptable as a sample by any reasonable standard. And that's all we strive for with Thoroughbred data also.

Ideally, you'll take a *random sample* to minimize or eliminate *bias* towards certain individuals, intended or not.

Random sampling means doing something like drawing lottery numbers printed on ping-pong balls which are continuously shuffled in an air-stirred drum.

The basic premise of random sampling is that *every individual in the population has an **equal chance** of being selected*. This is a crucial concept and must be remembered.

As simple as the above procedure sounds, *random samples* form the starting point of all valid statistical measurements. Now you know their meaning. There is nothing else to add.

Unfortunately, some researchers forget the necessity of random sampling and pay the penalty later by drawing false conclusions from data.

Applying the random-sample concept to Thoroughbred racing data, the population for a given horse is considered *hypothetical* rather than pre-existent as in the introductory example above.

That is, there really does not pre-exist a population of, say, times for running one mile on a fast track that one can randomly sample for a given horse like Whirlaway.

However, that does not change the essence of the population concept – either in importance or validity.

It simply means that, of *all the possible or theoretical races* a given horse *might have run* at a given distance on a given conditioned surface (fast, wet, slow, etc.) under a given range of weights, and so forth, you have *a single sample* already given to you by the horse itself – the one listed in his or her past-performance line of data in the DRFC.

Now is a good time to read Excursus E carefully and think about its implications. The concept of multiple random factors acting on a horse-rider team in each given race will pay great dividends for the remainder of this book. It is intended to help you understand more about statistics applied to this particular type of data.

For this study, each sample for a given horse is from its DRFC performance lines. These are the only data left by the horse for posterity to judge. These samples are generally small because, in most cases, they are far below thirty.

Thirty is a magic cutoff number separating small from large samples for most statistical purposes. The large-sample concept will not be discussed further. Suffice it to say that the DRFC samples are small.

It is sufficient for the reader to know that since, of necessity, small-sample statistics are used in this analysis, one must be more cautious with one's tests and conclusions. That is all. The conclusions will still be valid if the tests are carefully performed.

Some horses, in fact, run no more than 5 races in a given year. Ruffian is an outstanding example. Landaluce is another. Each ran only five races during her entire juvenile year. Ruffian's races were at 5.5 f and 6 f. Landaluce ran from 6 f to 8.5 f but still ran only five times.

Excursus E
Twelve Random Factors Acting
to Produce Race Outcome

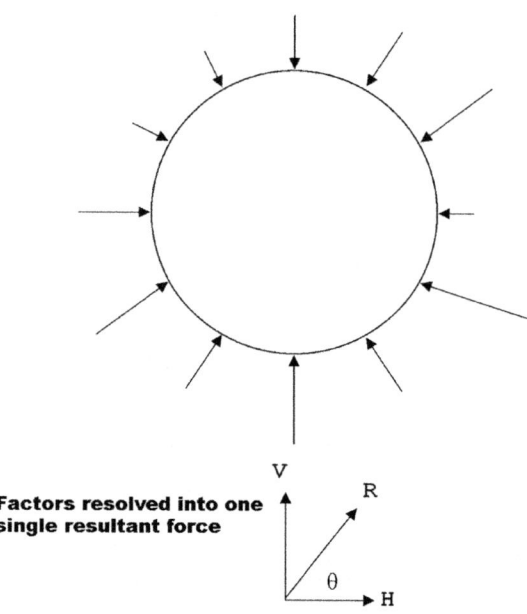

Factors resolved into one single resultant force

A physical analogy for the outcome of a race is given above by imagining a wooden or hard rubber disk on a smooth surface, as seen from directly above.

Twelve arrows pointing to the disk represent factors, known or unknown, which act on a given horse during a race and which determine the final time that horse runs. The time (direction the disk moves) is represented in the smaller diagram by R, the resultant force. It will be a ramdom variable under this set of conditions.

Basic trigonometry, not explained here, can be used to determine the horizontal and vertical components of each of the 12 forces. These resolve to two final components, H and V, whose resultant R has magnitude $\sqrt{(V^2 + H^2)}$.

The final time depends on exactly where R points. That direction, θ, is given by the relation $\text{Tan } \theta = V \div H$. Then $\theta = \text{Tan}^{-1}(V \div H)$.

These small samples will not lead to invalid results if they are analyzed properly with all assumptions openly stated.

Therefore, we generally have small samples of each horse's racing performance for a given year and age, and have noted that we assume each sample represents *one random sample* of many that *might have been drawn* from a hypothetical population of races the horse *might have run*.

Now we must meaningfully compare the samples with each other. The need to compare leads to the second of the basic concepts of statistics.

Concept 2: Sampling Distributions

Chart 2 shows an example of the most important distribution in statistics. It is called the Normal Distribution or bell curve due to its overall shape.

It will be used regularly throughout the remainder of this book, especially when making final comparisons using LA on the performance data to separate the horses at the highest level.

The normal distribution's important features are now presented so the reader can follow the ensuing data discussions.

Chart 2
The Normal Distribution and Standard Deviation

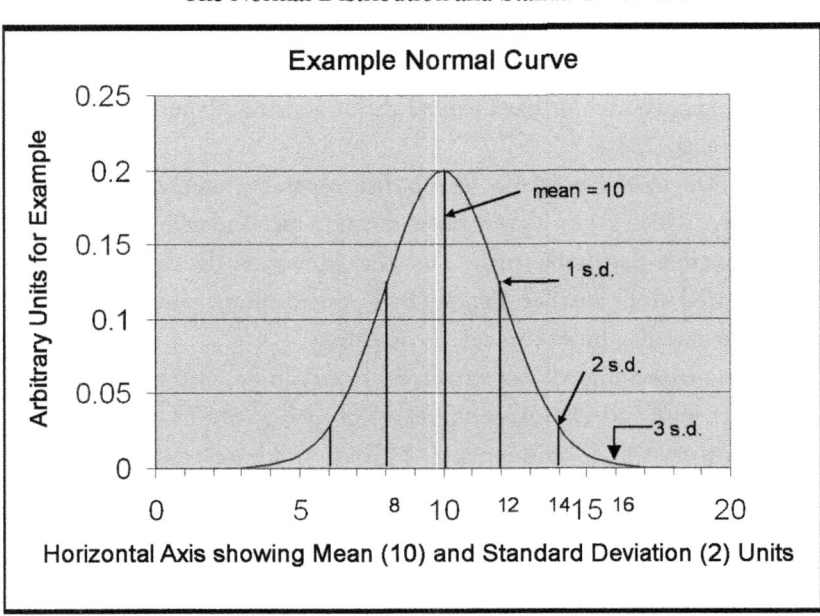

Chart 2 is one example of a normal curve. This curve accurately describes many samples or sets of measurements that are made on various groups or on objects in the real world, including Thoroughbred performance data.

The normal curve does not always perfectly fit the data. It does, however, often fit data closely enough that careful use of it will not introduce appreciable error. That is the key to the unbiased use of statistics. Where there is a danger of such error, or the magnitudes of those errors are known, they must be explained and justified.

There are, in fact, good tests for data normality. One is the Shapiro-Wilk Test (S-W), developed in 1965. The S-W was used to determine the normalcy, or lack thereof, for *each distribution of data used in this study* before comparing those data.

The goal was to use only individual performance data that was undistorted and unbiased. Statistics is intended to give unbiased comparisons, but it is sometimes carelessly applied without regard for its limitations. Such use is undoubtedly what led Prime Minister Disraeli to cast the aspersion quoted previously.

The normal distribution in Chart 2 follows an exact mathematical equation, but it would not help the reader to know the equation for that curve, and so it will be omitted. It can be found in most standard statistics texts. *Statistical Analysis with Excel for Dummies* (19) is an excellent beginning reference for both general statistics and Excel. Although the title is facetiously condescending, the book provides a good, thorough introduction to the topic.

Four features of the normal curve are most important: (1) it is centered about a value called the *mean or average value,* (2) a number called the *standard deviation* is associated with it; (3) it is symmetrical around the mean, each side being a mirror image of the other, and (4) its height at each point on the horizontal axis shows the relative number of sample values occurring at that point.

It is critical to understand that each area under the normal curve between *consecutive* standard deviation points (marked by vertical lines on the graph in Chart 2) contains an *exact, known proportion of the total area under the entire curve!*

To simplify Chart 2, only the value 8 (representing -1SD) below the mean was shown. However, the remaining values, 6 and 2, are symmetrical around the mean just as are the values *14* and *16* above the mean.

The area between the mean and the *first* standard deviation *on either side* of the mean is 34.13%. The area between the first and *second* standard deviations on either side of the mean is 13.59%, and the area from the second to the *third* standard deviation on either side of the mean is 2.14%.

When these percentages are added, one finds that approximately 0.27% of the area beneath the curve is unaccounted for. This means that 0.135% remains *beyond* the *third* standard deviation on either side of the mean.

For practical purposes, and especially for analyzing Thoroughbred performance data, these areas are irrelevant to accuracy and will not be considered in this study.

That is, they represent cases so rare that it would prove nothing to include them with respect to comparing the performance of two or more given horses.

Mean and Standard Deviation

The mean and standard deviation will now be described. These two statistics and the areas under the normal curve are really all that need be understood to see how the normal curve is used, especially for LA.

Concept 3: Mean

Many readers already know how to calculate a *mean* or *average*. However, it does not hurt to reconsider the process for those new to statistics.

Suppose we have past performance data for Horse A which gives her times for three races of 6 f each on a fast rated track. The weights she carried in each race are also given, and they are close enough so that we don't suspect they appreciably altered her performance in any one race as compared with the others. The exact effect of weight will be discussed later in detail.

Given the above conditions, we can find a valid mean or average time for her for these three performances by just adding the individual times and dividing by three. For easy calculation, assume her times were 65, 66 and 67 s – pretty fast for 6 f.

Her average or mean time for the three races is:

$$\text{Mean} = x_{av} = (65 + 66 + 67) \div 3 = 198 \div 3 = 66.$$

This relatively fast-and-easy procedure is how one always calculates the arithmetic mean or average of a set of measurements. Simply add the measurements and then divide by the total number of measurements.

Concept 4: Standard Deviation

The *standard deviation* is really just another kind of average. However, it is a bit more complicated in that it involves some subtractions, squares and square roots. Refer to the complete example given in Excursus D.

Qualitatively, one determines the standard deviation by first calculating the sample average. Then subtract the average from *each separate value* of the original data. This gives a set of what statisticians call *deviation scores*.

There will be as many deviation scores, three in this case, as there are sample values.

A deviation score is found simply by determining how much each individual score or measurement in the sample *deviates* (is different from) the average value of the sample.

Each deviation score is then squared, and these squared terms are added. The result is then divided by the number of measurements minus 1, (n – 1).

The number of measurements is called the *sample size*. It is denoted either by n or N. One less than the sample size is then denoted by either n-1 or N-1.

After dividing the sum of the squared deviation scores by n -1, take the square root of the result, and the standard deviation, SD, is obtained.

Both positive and negative standard deviations are produced since every square root has, by definition, two answers – one plus and one minus. These are denoted by the symbol ±. The standard deviation is, as stated previously, a type of average of the deviation scores of all the sample measurements.

It is interesting that, for a normal or near-normal distribution, the standard deviation delimits the precise areas under the normal curve previously given.

The example above, with the three times of 65, 66 and 67 s was too simple to give an interesting and/or meaningful SD. If you follow the outlined steps for calculating the SD (as hereafter abbreviated) the value(s) ±1.00 are obtained.

Many inexpensive pocket calculators directly give means, standard deviations, squares and square roots simply by entering a number and then pressing the appropriately marked key.

To review, the square of a number is the result obtained when the number is multiplied by itself.

The square root of a number is the number such that *when it is multiplied by itself* returns the original number. Thus squares and square roots are inverses.

Example: 6 squared is 6 x 6 = 36. It is also denoted as 6^2. The square root of 36, denoted $\sqrt{36}$, is plus or minus (±) 6 because 6 x 6 = 36 and -6 x -6 = 36.

Concept 5: Skewness and Kurtosis

Skewness: It was just explained that a normal distribution is symmetrical around its mean value. When a set of data is skewed, it means simply that more values are bunched together on one side of the mean than on the other. Thus, the distribution does not have mirror-image symmetry around its central vertical axis.

Since a picture is worth a thousand words, or perhaps more, Chart 3 shows a skewed distribution.

Chart 3
A distribution skewed to the right.

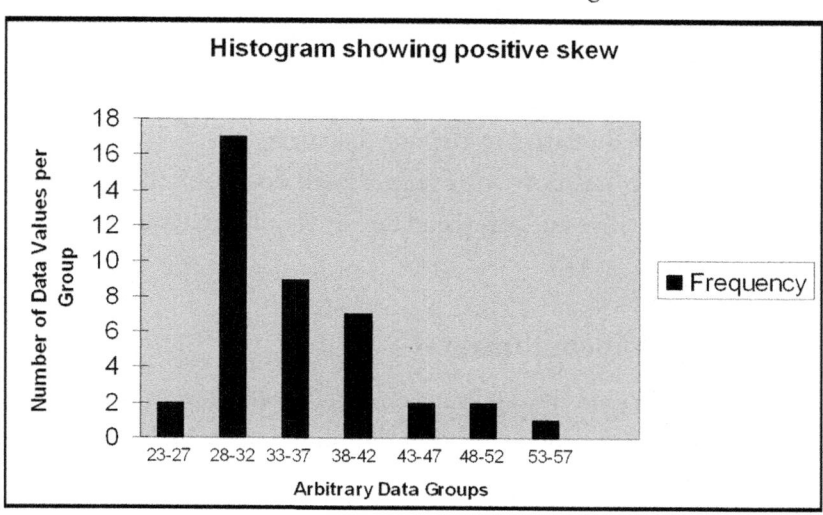

Chart 3 shows a *positively skewed* distribution. If you compare Chart 3 with the normal distribution in Chart 2, it appears that the peak has been shifted to the left and more data values are shifted to the right.

The histogram shown actually has a mean of 34.7 and an SD of 7.2.

Distributions can also be *negatively skewed*. In that case the *tail* portion is on the left side and the peak is on the right side – opposite to the figure in Chart 3.

There is a convenient statistical test for skewness in Excel that is named, appropriately, SKEW. It gives a mathematical value for the amount of skewness. For comparison, a normal distribution has zero skewness.

When the SKEW test is run on the data in the above histogram, a value of +1.305 is obtained. The positive value indicates that the data are skewed to the right.

Skewness will be referred to later when testing the performance data of the various horses finishing high in the data sorts is discussed.

Kurtosis: Kurtosis means how peaked or flattened a given distribution is compared to the normal curve. A standard normal curve has a kurtosis of three. The histogram shown in Chart 3 above has a calculated kurtosis of +1.425 using Excel's KURT function. This number is actually the *excess kurtosis* beyond the standard value, 3.

A positive kurtosis, such as this value, means the distribution has a higher peak than the normal curve, and a negative kurtosis means it is flattened or lowered relative to the normal curve.

It is clear that the above histogram's peak does look like it has been both pushed to the left and stretched upward compared with the normal curve's peak.

Concept 6: Confidence Interval

The confidence interval gives the *range of values, for a given percent probability,* that you would expect the sample mean to fall between if you took a large number of samples and calculated a mean for each sample.

Recall that the sample of data for any given horse, as given by DRFC, is only one of a theoretically infinite number of data samples for the given distances that the horse might have run.

For example, suppose the horse had run ten one-mile races on tracks rated fast while carrying a limited range of weights between 125 lb and 130 lb.

Given these conditions, we can reasonably say that the races were run under equivalent conditions and that they represent the horse's true ability at running one mile.

Assume you were only allowed to draw a random sample of five results from these races for analysis.

How many samples of five could actually be drawn given the ten possible choices of races the horse actually ran?

The answer is given by a mathematical formula which won't be analyzed in detail. However, the results will perhaps be surprising.

The formula is for the number of combinations of *n* items taken *r* at a time; it is symbolized $_nC_r$. In this case n = 10 and r = 5. That is, the horse ran 10 races and you're sampling five.

Many hand-held calculators can compute this number using only a few key strokes.

When the values are substituted in the formula and the calculator crunches the numbers, the result is 252! This means it was possible to have drawn any one of 252 samples of five values from the ten values for times the horse actually posted for one-mile races.

However, assume this *particular sample* has a mean of 93.40 s. This is a decent speed for one mile. In fact, the value was chosen because it was the time posted by Secretariat for the mile in winning the 1973 Gotham Stakes. It is used here as an example, but it represents a realistic value.

How confident can one be that a mean from a single sample truly represents the horse's ability to run one mile under reasonably identical conditions?

To determine this, calculate a **confidence interval** (CI). Use the formula: $CI = x \pm z_c \cdot s_x$. In this formula, x is the value just calculated for the mean, 93.4 s.

To this value, add or subtract the expression $z_c \cdot s_x$, where z_c is found from a table of z scores for the desired confidence interval, and s_x is the standard error of the mean.

It is easiest simply to state that for a 95% confidence interval around the mean of a normal distribution, z_c is 1.96. This value comes from the characteristic spread of the standard normal curve.

The value of s_x is found directly from the sample by dividing the sample's SD by the square root of the sample size, in this case 5. The formula is:

$$s_x = SD \div \sqrt{n}.$$

Assume the sample had an SD of 0.25 s. The square root of 5 is 2.24 to two decimal places.

Then 0.25 ÷ 2.24 is 0.11, again using two-decimal-place accuracy.

Therefore, the 95% confidence interval for the sample is:

$$93.40 \text{ s} \pm (1.96 \times 0.11) = 93.40 \text{ s} \pm 0.22 \text{ s}.$$

Subtracting 0.22 s from 93.40 s gives the lower value of the confidence interval, 93.18 s; adding 0.22 s gives the upper value, 93.62 s.

The 95% CI for this example means that if one could draw 100 random samples of five values each from the original set of ten race results, the sample's mean value would be within this range for 95% of the cases.

The idea of confidence intervals will be used sparingly in analyzing the DRFC data, but this is an important statistical concept to remember.

Concept 7: Variance

Stated simply, variance is the square of the standard deviation. Since it is a square, it is always positive.

When standard deviation was discussed earlier and its derivation was given in Excursus D, it was stated that SD values are both positive and negative.

Positive SD values refer to sample measurements *above* the mean, and negative SD values refer to sample measurements *below* the mean.

Negative square roots are easily understood. If you have a number such as 9 and are asked to take its square root, just remember to first find the numerical value and then attach a plus or minus sign, ±, to it, as required.

For instance, the square root of 9, symbolized $\sqrt{9}$, is technically ± 3, and not just 3.

The algebraic reason is that two minus numbers multiplied together, like -3·-3, give a positive result by definition! Therefore, $(-3) \cdot (-3) = 9$. A number such as 9 with no sign before it is always assumed positive. This is easier than always writing +9 when the result is the same.

The concept of plus-or-minus values is what Excursus D is representing in a kind of abbreviated form -- that standard deviation comes in both varieties. The numerical result is identical for both cases.

Why is variance important? To perform the final two tests I'll now explain, the variance must be used. These tests are needed to test hypotheses about two or more samples, and they form the heart and soul of what is called *inferential* statistics.

Inferential statistics allows making valid statements about whether one population *differs significantly* from another while having only a limited sample from each. This concept is extremely useful for comparing Thoroughbred racing data.

When the data from two horses are compared to judge which horse is better at a given distance, what we are actually doing statistically is asking whether there is a *significant difference* between the means of the two populations from which their samples came. This is highly important to remember! **Significant difference in statistical language implies better or worse, in qualitative terms, regarding Thoroughbred performance.**

Concept 8: F test

The F test is named for a famous statistician, Sir Ronald Aylmer Fisher, its developer. The F test and the so-called *Student's t test*, explained in the next section, form the core of statistical testing.

The F test is performed by taking the ratio of two variances. Where do the two variances originate? They are the squares of the standard deviations of the two samples one is comparing.

To illustrate, suppose you have two samples you want to compare – to determine whether they differ significantly. Assume that the first consists of five values of the times that Horse A ran five separate one-mile races. Let the second sample consist of seven values of the times that Horse B ran seven separate one-mile races.

Assume that no reason exists to think the track surfaces or any other aspect of these races favored one horse or the other, and a scientific judgment concerning whether one horse was significantly faster (better) for the mile than the other is desired.

A t-test can determine this, but an F-test should first be done because the two tests are interrelated and interdependent. The nice thing is that Excel does both tests easily.

Depending on whether the variances of the two samples are equal or *significantly different*, the t-test could give different answers to the question about whether one horse was significantly faster than the other – assuming, of course, that their times are sufficiently close to begin with. Otherwise it is nearly obvious without the tests!

Equal variances are preferable because they provide a better estimate of t values. However, Excel accommodates both equal and unequal variances with the t test.

Assume, then, that Horse A's sample SD is 0.35 s and that Horse B's sample SD is 0.45 s.

First find the variances of each sample by squaring each of their SD values. This gives 0.1225 for Horse A and 0.2025 for Horse B.

The ratio of the *larger* to the smaller variance (always taken in that order) is F and is 0.2025/0.1225 = 1.6531.

The value 1.6531 can now be used in FDIST to obtain the value 0.3261. This represents the probability of obtaining the F value just calculated if there was no difference between the sample variances.

Since variance tests are not considered significant if F is greater than 0.05, the above result is considered not significant, since it is greater than 0.05.

That is, from this data one cannot say that the larger of the variances is significantly greater than the smaller variance, given the sample sizes.

Concept 9: Student's T-test

Having performed the F-test and found that the variances do not differ significantly, the t-test can now be performed. William S. Gosset developed this test in 1908, using the pseudonym *Student*, because the Guinness Brewery in Dublin, Ireland, where he was employed, held proprietary rights on his work.

The t-test is one of the most basic and yet powerful tests within statistics. It allows comparing, among other things, two samples and determining whether they differ significantly. It does this by mathematically determining whether their means could differ as much as they do by pure chance or whether something else caused the difference – like an actual difference in ability between the horses!

For this example, let the two samples represent five separate data values for Horse C and Horse D obtained under reasonably identical conditions. We wish to determine whether one horse was significantly better on this measurement or whether they were essentially equivalent.

The most straightforward way to explain how the t-test works, as it is used on the DRFC data, is by example.

Run Excel's t-test on the two data samples using the values listed in Table 5 below.

Table 5

Two small samples compared with the t-test

Sample 1 Values (Horse C)	Sample 2 Values (Horse D)	t-test result	Sample 3 Values
9.40	10.40	$\alpha = 0.481$	12.39
7.44	8.44		10.44
10.49	11.49	interpretation:	13.48
12.55	13.55	not significant	15.55
12.40	13.40		15.39
mean = 10.46 SD = 2.14 variance = 4.59	mean = 11.46 SD = 2.14 variance = 4.59		t-test result: $\alpha = 0.057$

One distribution, from which Sample 1 was taken, had a mean of 10 and a SD of 2. The second distribution, from which sample 2 was randomly drawn, had a mean of 11 and a SD of 2.

Chart 4 shows the normal distributions corresponding to the populations from which samples 1 and 2 were drawn.

Chart 4
Comparison of two normal curves with means 10 and 11.

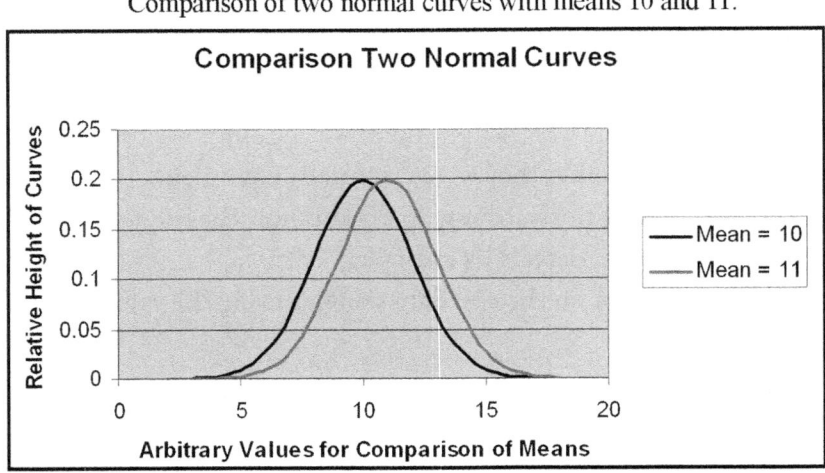

The t-test (run in Excel using command, TTEST) does a mathematical calculation that tells whether the distance between the means (10 and 11) in this example is considered significant, considering the individual values which were sampled from the two populations and were listed in Table 5, columns 1 and 2.

Concept 10: Significance Level, alpha

In this case, the value for t results in a probability of 0.481 that the two samples could have come from the same population. In other words, these two samples **are not considered significantly different.**

The value 0.481 is called *alpha*, and is denoted by the small Greek letter α. Generally, alpha values between 0.05 and 0.01 or less are considered significant.

Since 0.481 is greater than 0.05, it is not statistically significant.

The technical protocol of statistics requires that, before running a t-test, what is called the *null hypothesis*, denoted by H_0, must be stated. The null hypothesis assumes there is *no difference* between the means of the two populations (running times of two horses being compared) from which samples were taken.

The objective is to determine whether to accept or reject the null hypothesis. Acceptance or rejection is equivalent to saying that one horse is or is not better than the other. *Note carefully* that statistics **never** tells you whether or not the null hypothesis is **true or false.**

That is, it never implies that one horse is or is not better than another. It simply indicates whether one should accept or reject the null hypothesis concerning the significance of the difference between two means based on the probability of finding a difference as large as, or larger than, the one found in the given sample.

The *alternate hypothesis*, denoted by H_1, states that there *is a significant difference* between the two population means (horses' running times). This hypothesis must be accepted if the null hypothesis is rejected. The two are complementary, and there are no other hypotheses available. That is how statistical hypothesis testing is designed.

Statistical tests advise going one way or another, and the experimenter must decide whether to accept or reject the advice.

To repeat, never, based on the t test or any other statistical test, say that you have **proven** one horse better or worse than another. That is the type of misinterpretation that gives statistics much of its ill-deserved bad reputation. It is generally not statistics that is at fault, but the statistical interpreter.

Running the t-test will give the *probability of having a difference as great as the one observed* **if the samples came from the same population.**

If the probability is *greater than* 0.05, as it was in the example above, then one usually says that the samples could have come from the same population – or the horses seemed equivalent, to put the result in racing terms.

If the probability is 0.05 or less, then one can be 95% confident (1.00 – 0.05 = 0.95, which is then multiplied by 100 and called a percent) that the samples came from different populations (i.e., one horse's times tested significantly different from the other's).

In that case, the test result *is* statistically significant. We call alpha the *level of significance* of the t-test. It is also termed the probability of making a Type I error, but that does not warrant further discussion here.

Although Table 5 lists the two sample means as 10.46 and 11.46, the numbers were, in fact, samples generated randomly by Excel from normal populations having means of 10 and 11 and SDs 2.00. The difference is simply due to the randomness of the sampling.

This is an important example of the fact that small samples from even known normal distributions – computer generated in this case – do not generally give the exact values that characterize those same distributions.

Chart 5 shows where three normal distributions having means of 10, 11 and 13 and standard deviations 2.00 fall relative to each other. It is easy to see graphically how t tests become significant as the distance between means of the three distributions increases.

Chart 5
Three Overlapped Normal Distributions

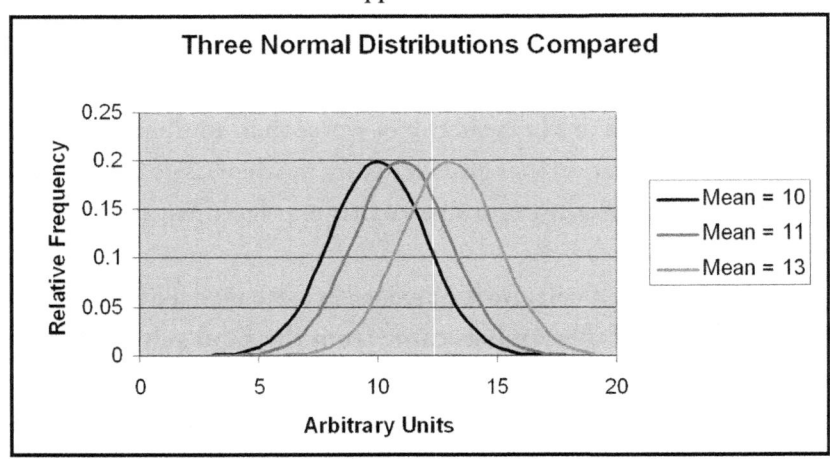

The five sample results from the third population, represented by the rightmost curve in Chart 5, are listed in column 4 of Table 5.

In this case, the difference in the means between sample 1 and sample 3 is nearly significant because α is only slightly larger than 0.05. For practical reasons, we probably would interpret it as significant if we were comparing the times of two horses for running the same distance repeatedly.

Linear Trend Analysis

The final topic necessary for understanding the individual analyses done in this book is Linear Trend Analysis, LTA.

A linear trend is simply a straight line which the computer fits to some data points. Trend Analysis is simply the method for interpreting the trend line based on three primary numbers. Statisticians give trend analysis the fancier name *regression analysis*.

The LTA method is now illustrated by presenting Kelso's data for 1961. The great champion, ranked fourth by BHI and second in the present 3YO sort, was then four years old.

Only three numbers need be understood regarding linear trends. Once you understand them, you can easily interpret what all linear trend lines mean. These numbers refer to the *slope*, the *intercept* and the COD, or R^2, for the trend line.

When you use Excel to determine the linear trend of a set of data points, it automatically supplies all three numbers for you, plus seven you don't always use!

Kelso Example and Application

As listed in DRFC, Kelso ran nine races in 1961 at age four.

Some key information pertinent to understanding his overall performance is also included.

Table 6
Kelso's basic race data for 1961 – age 4

Date	Track	Surface	Weight (lb)	Distance (mi)	Time (s)	Finish	Margin
5/19	Aqu	fast	124	0.875	84.0	1st	1.5
5/30	Aqu	fast	130	1.00	95.6	1st	Neck
6/17	Bel	fast	130	1.125	108.0	2nd	Head
7/4	Aqu	fast	133	1.25	122.0	1st	5
7/22	Aqu	fast	136	1.25	121.6	1st	1.25
9/4	AP	good	132	1.00	94.6	4th	5.75

Table 6 – continued

9/30	Bel	fast	126	1.25	120.0	1st	8
10/21	Aqu	fast	124	2.00	205.8	1st	5
11/11	Lrl	firmT*	126	1.5	146.2	2nd	0.75

*Notation explained in text

Kelso's races for 1961 are listed in chronological order, top to bottom. His final race for that year was on turf, the only such race on that surface throughout the year.

That it was a turf race is denoted by the letter T after the track condition, *firm*.

Two linear trends were run on Kelso's data. The first *did not include the turf race*, but the second did. The results for both make an informative comparison.

To perform LTA on the data in Table 6 using Excel, enter the data for the distances run (this group of related data is called an *array* by Excel) in a single column. In the adjacent column *to the right* on the Excel spreadsheet, enter the corresponding time data. This is called the time array. The distance data must be entered to the *left of* and *adjacent to* the time data for Excel to run LTA.

Next, select a two-column by five-row group of cells in which to put Excel's linear trend results. This is simply the protocol that the program LINEST requires.

Next, click the f_x button and select *LINEST* from the drop-down menu.

After defining the range of cells in which the data reside on the spreadsheet, for example B2:C9, press **Shift-Ctrl-Enter**, and the trend coefficients appear in the 2 x 5 cell array you first selected. It's just that easy!

Two adjacent columns appear which have five numbers in each. *Only three of these are really of immediate importance for explaining the basic principles of trend analysis.* They are the top numbers in both columns and the third number down the left column.

When Kelso's data for just the first eight races of 1961 are analyzed using LINEST, these numbers are: 109.28, -14.13, and 0.9983, to four decimal places.

The number 109.28 (rounded to two decimal places) is the *slope* of the straight line that best fits the data. The second number, -14.13, is where the straight line would theoretically cross the time axis (the vertical axis of the graph) if the distance run was zero. This is obviously irrelevant to real data.

Since zero distance is never involved, consider this number mainly as a *locator* for the leftmost point on the line. Since *only two points are needed to completely determine a straight line*, the intercept and slope are all one needs.

Chart 6 shows the actual result when Excel plots the straight line or trend line.

CHART 6
Kelso's Trend Line for 1961 (turf race not included)

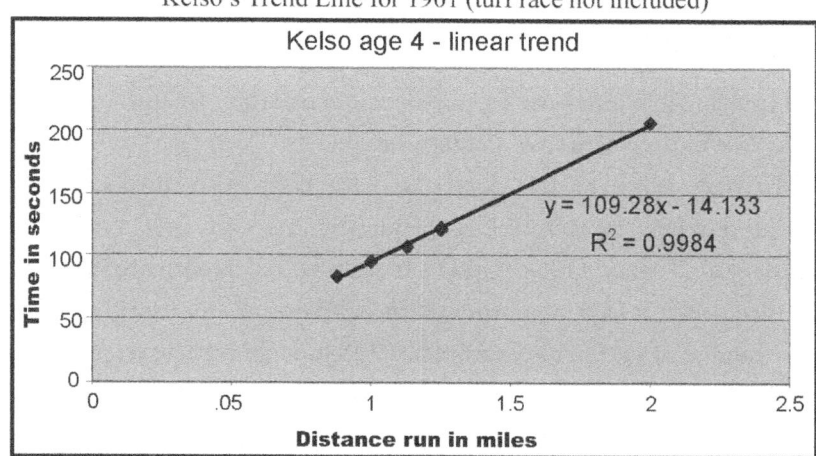

Notice that the three numbers discussed on the previous page appear in the right margin of Chart 6.

The first two are simply part of an equation, namely, $\hat{y} = 109.28x - 14.133$, where $\hat{y}$ means a predicted value.

This equation "tells" you to pick any distance x for which Kelso might have run, so long as it is between the original data limits on the line's horizontal axis, and it will predict his time, $\hat{y}$, for you based on x.

These distance limits are 0.875 mi, his shortest race of 1961, and 2.00 mi, his longest race. If you do this, the equation will accurately predict how long he would have taken to run the given distance.

If one asks, for example, how long Kelso would likely have taken to run a 1.375-mi, or 11-f race, simply substitute 1.375 for x in the formula. Then multiply that value of x by 109.28 and subtract 14.133, just as the formula states. The answer is 136.13 s, rounded to two decimal places.

This is the predicted time, indicated as ŷ by statisticians and pronounced "y-hat," in which Kelso would have run 11 f that year based on the given data. He never actually ran that distance, but you can see from the graph that it is logical to assume he would have been close to that value, all other factors remaining equal.

A final piece of information is that the slope number, 109.28, means that Kelso's times increased by 109.28 s for every *unit increase*, in this case one mile, in distance that he ran.

That's all the slope means. It is the *increase in vertical distance* of the trend line *for each unit increase in horizontal distance. In other words, it is the increase in time with unit distance run.*

The best, however, has been saved for last! The third number is associated with the symbol R^2. Statisticians call that symbol the *Coefficient of Determination (COD)*. It sounds like a mouthful and quite intellectual, but it is easy to understand and eminently useful.

The value of R^2 in this example, 0.9984, or 99.84% when converted to percentage units, as is more usual, means that the computer-generated trend line accurately explains 99.84 percent of Kelso's changes in running time based on the changes in distance that he ran!

This represents a nearly perfect mathematical fit of the trend line to the data.

Surprisingly, and fortunately, the majority of the trend lines analyzed for the horses in this study fit their data with greater than 99 percent accuracy.

This means that it is *extremely safe to make predictions from such a line*, provided one does not extend it much beyond its actual original boundaries.

It is probable that one could *interpolate* (use shorter distances) or *extrapolate* (use longer distances) than the trend line originally was based on to a furlong or two in either direction, but not much farther, if you wished to remain accurate in predicting performance at such distances.

There are calculations of confidence intervals one can perform to give an idea of the error involved in these interpolations and extrapolations, but they become involved beyond the level needed for this book.

In fact, only one LTA interpolation is performed later in this text, and its results and their likely error are explained when it is presented.

If the data for the final turf race are added to that just discussed and a second trend analysis is run, the new prediction equation becomes: $\hat{y} = 108.32x - 13.327$.

You can see that this differs slightly, though not unreasonably, from the original equation. Such changes in trend equations invariably occur when even one data point is changed. You must remember this.

That is why care must be taken, especially when analyzing small samples, as are common for the data discussed herein.

More important than the equation alone, however, is the new value for R^2. It becomes 0.9975. This scarcely differs from the first COD, and it means that the changed equation still accurately predicts 99.75% of the changes in running times as they are influenced by changes in distance run.

Therefore, including Kelso's single turf race did not unreasonably contaminate the data originally analyzed for purely dirt races, as many might argue.

This example should help silence another charge often made by critics – that even surfaces rated the same can't really be analyzed as if they were. If one cannot do this, with appropriate caution, one is virtually helpless regarding Thoroughbred data analysis!

We are now equipped to apply actual data analyses and see what they tell us about the greatest horse of all.

CHAPTER 7

We cannot catch the fleeting minute and put it alongside a later minute.
-- Arthur Milne

General Linear Trend Analysis Results

The first layer of the data sieve, sorting by fourteen categories, is accomplished. Twenty horses, plus ties, from both the 2YO and 3YO age brackets now advance to the second stage of analysis – LTA.

It is crucial to remember that none of the data in this study were subjected to any so-called transformations or modifications.

The pure past-performance-line data (often called "raw scores") from the DRFC were analyzed using only the simplest and most common statistical tests.

To reemphasize a comment made near the beginning of this book, the only way that Thoroughbred racing data can be studied scientifically is via valid statistical analysis.

These types of analyses are used, for example, by physicists studying the nature of the universe via the interactions of sub-atomic particles. This may surprise the many readers distrustful of statistics.

Statistics is used within physics to double-check that no spurious or biased results are reported. It is ironic, as an understatement, that some readers of this book will claim biased results simply because their favorite horse was not selected – all statistical validity aside.

If he or she was not selected, it is because the numbers laid down forever by the performance of those particular horses simply did not rank high enough to advance beyond the preliminary sort.

Those points now clarified, we proceed to the second layer of the data sieve – LTA of the 2YO and 3YO data.

Trend Analysis Considerations

From the previous overview of trend analysis, you recall that *three key numbers* are produced by Excel when the LINEST routine is run on a set of data.

For all LTA applications herein, the data sets have only two variables.

The first variable, called the *independent* variable, is the *distance* a horse ran for each race in a given year. Distance is always plotted along the horizontal axis of its chart or graph.

The second variable, called the *dependent* variable, is the *time* a horse required to run each of the given distances. Time is always plotted along the vertical axis of its chart or graph.

The variables are given these names because the independent variable (distances, x) can be set beforehand. That is, distance is controllable in the sense that humans decide how long a given race will be.

The dependent variable (running times, y) will then depend on the distance for which it is measured. It cannot be controlled.

It's up to the horse and rider to use up time, record time, or however one wishes to express passing time during a race, depending on the horse's ability to run the pre-determined distance and the jockey' skill in motivating him and outmaneuvering the other horses.

Microsoft Excel functions best when **independent** variables are entered in a column *adjacent to and immediately left* of the **dependent** variable when they are placed in spreadsheet cells.

When the trend results of LINEST are graphed (charted, graphed or plotted are all acceptable terms), Excel places the independent variable, distance, along the horizontal axis and the dependent variable, time, is placed along the vertical axis. This is just a mathematical tradition.

For historical reasons, the independent variable is often designated "x," while the dependent variable is designated "y." This study preserves that format.

These variables might just as logically have been symbolized by "h" for horizontal and "v" for vertical! The letters are merely symbolic with no meaning beyond that.

Thus, as one views a typical chart or graph, distances (x) increase from left to right and times (y) increase from bottom to top of the chart.

Chart 7 is an additional example of what was just stated. It represents Sir Barton's linear trend (regression line) for his 3YO campaign of 1919, and it provides a good example of the concepts needed for understanding the linear trend portion of the data analyses.

CHART 7
Linear Trend Results for Sir Barton
Age 3 - 1919

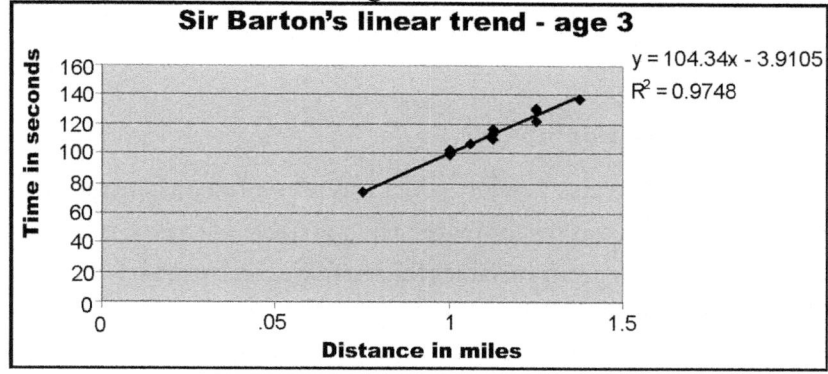

Chart 7 is quite revealing. For one thing, it includes all thirteen of Sir Barton's 1919 races. These races were on six different tracks and were run under widely different track conditions.

Only *five* of the races were run on tracks rated *fast*. *Two* efforts were on surfaces rated *heavy*; *two* were on tracks rated *sloppy*; *two* were on *good* surfaces; *one* was on a *slow* surface and the *other* was on a surface classified as *muddy*.

You see that Sir Barton by no means had easy running for much of his sophomore year.

Yet the trend line in Chart 7 shows remarkable uniformity and an R^2 value indicating that nearly 97.5% of Sir Barton's variation in running time per race was accounted for or explainable simply by the increase in distance he ran.

Another way of saying this is that the trend line fits the data with 97.5% accuracy and is an excellent predictor.

One might have expected a less accurate fit of the line to the data since Sir Barton's running conditions varied greatly.

It is undoubtedly more a compliment to Sir Barton's athletic ability than anything else that his trend line shows such a uniform fit to the data. It also makes a strong case for using the linear trend technique to separate the better horses who survived the initial sort.

The majority of their races were on tracks rated fast. However, from what has been shown for Sir Barton's data, track condition apparently makes far less difference than many pundits would normally argue as far as generating accurate trend lines or comparing horses is concerned.

Bias and Correlation

Sir Barton's data also reinforce the ideas presented earlier concerning the correlation between two or more racing variables. That is, correlation coefficients between given variables fluctuate widely from horse to horse, as Tables 2.B.a through 2.B.c show.

Therefore, it is not necessarily true that a given sort category such as weight, track conditions or any other factor chosen for sorting definitely favored one horse over another. It apparently all depends on the horse!

This presents a strong argument against those who argue that the 2YO and 3YO sorts were unfair, lopsided, biased, etc.

Any preference that one or two sort categories may have shown to a given horse was probably more than compensated with respect to all forty-four BHI horses ranked.

There is no absolutely scientific way to screen horses, but so long as each category represents an acknowledged parameter that is important to racing, as each of the sort categories can claim, they are thus **unbiased within reasonable expectations.**

It is important historically, as alluded to previously, that three of the races included in Chart 7 would eventually become known as the Triple Crown. They were not classified under that title in 1919 when Sir Barton won them and would not be so classified until Omaha won them in 1935, as was discussed earlier.

When Sir Barton ran them, the Kentucky Derby was 1.25 mi (10 f), as it has been since 1896. However, the Preakness was 1.125 mi (9 f) rather than its present 1.1875 mi (9.5 f); the Belmont was 1.375 mi (11 f) rather than today's more challenging 1.5 mi (12 f).

Extending Trend Line Limits

A question invariably arises about extending trend lines derived using statistical applications such as LINEST to regions beyond the original data. Now is a good time for discussion, since it was alluded to previously.

This practice is, at best, risky. Most researchers shun it like the Plague! Even when the linear trend fits the given data accurately, as is the case for all horses in this study, it can be subject to more error than one may imagine.

The following example is based on Secretariat's trend line, based on his 3YO races. You decide.

Discussion of Secretariat's "Blowout"

Fortunately, a complete log of Secretariat's training is available, in the excellent twenty-fifth anniversary commemorative book by Raymond G. Woolfe, Jr. (20). It shows that on Wednesday March 14, 1973, as a very young 3YO and before fame touched him, Secretariat did a 3 f workout, termed "freakish" by the author, in 32.60 s.

The question now is how accurately would Secretariat's LTA for his later 3YO races predict ("post-dict" is a more appropriate term) that time for that particular distance?

When the distance 0.375 miles (3 f) is substituted for x in Secretariat's linear trend equation, $102.669x - 7.918$, the predicted running time is $\hat{y} = 30.58$ s.

Since his actual running time for the workout was 32.60 s, the error is slightly over 6%. This is not a glaring error, and of course Secretariat was even less mature when he ran the 3 f than after his 3YO campaign.

By the end of the 1973 season, as a mature 3YO, Secretariat may well have been able to run 3 f in 30.58 s, especially since his jockey, Ron Turcotte, nearly always said he held him back.

In comparison, the world record for 3 f, as of 2005, is 31.01 s. It was set by Eclat, age 5, at Remington Park on Monday November 28, 2005. He carried 123 lb.

When you realize that Secretariat's linear trend fits the *given* data with 99.44 percent accuracy, you see what price may be paid in predictability, even for this high level of R^2.

We are trying to extend Secretariat's linear trend *four furlongs* below the shortest distance, 7 f, on which his original trend line was based, and that is definitely ill-considered. With a half-mile distance differential, we've exceeded the limits of truly accurate predictability.

In closing, Secretariat's standard error of estimate (STEYX) from his trend line is 1.88. The above prediction error represents 1.07 of one standard error. It is, therefore, well within the predictable limits of error which extend to ± 3 STEYX.

It is likely that, for the cases in this study, one could confidently extend a given linear trend to distances of one-half to one furlong on either side of the original boundary limits without incurring significant error.

This will, in fact, cautiously be done later in comparing Ruffian's and Landaluce's 2YO trend lines.

Comment on Calculations for Non-Winning Times

One final important and slightly specialized calculation must now be explained, because it has been used in this study. After that, the trend analyses for the finalist horses in both the 2YO and 3YO age categories are presented.

This specialized calculation concerns how running time was determined in this study for a horse that did *not win* but finished within a half-dozen or so lengths of the winner. These non-winning times were necessary for speed and momentum calculations used in the initial data sorts.

Finishing second or third (placing or showing) happens enough even for the champion horses in this study to require consideration and discussion.

One inconvenience of the DRFC data is that it gives only the finish time for the winner of a given race. It does usually tell *how many lengths behind* the winner a particular horse whose past-performance data is being analyzed finished, because it gives the margins of the place and show horses.

Since we also need a final time for the non-winning horse in order to determine his or her trend line, the following procedure was devised and used as necessary:

For explanatory reasons alone, assume the winning horse ran one mile in 95.0 s while the particular horse in question finished second, *three lengths* back.

Let one length equal eight feet, as is commonly done in racing calculations. Then being three lengths back when the winner crossed the finish line is the same as being twenty-four feet short of having run the total distance of one mile.

That is, it is 5,280 ft minus 24 ft or 5,256 ft. Thus, the second-place horse ran 5,256 ft in 95.0 s, the time in which the winner finished the entire race.

Therefore, divide 5,256 ft by 95.0 s (the winning time at official end of race) and obtain 55.33 ft/s as the *second-place* horse's average speed to **that point**. The winner's speed was actually 5,280ft ÷ 95 s = 55.58 ft/s, which makes sense.

Further assume that the second-place horse maintained the same average speed for the **remaining** 24 ft he or she had to run to reach the finish line. This is a reasonable assumption for top Thoroughbreds covering such a relatively short distance, especially as they strive for their best finish.

There may be a small inherent error in this assumption, but there is no other way to approximate a non-winning time.

For instance, it was found that, both in Man o' War's loss to Upset at 6 f and Secretariat's loss in his maiden race at 5.5 f, both horses *decelerated* slightly in the last fractional mile. However, the amount of deceleration over half a dozen or so lengths should not significantly change the results presented here.

The above caution being stated, calculate the time taken to cover the remaining 24 ft, *assuming constant speed*, by dividing 24 ft by 55.33 ft/s and obtain 0.43 s. This represents the **minimum** extra fractional time the second-place horse needed to reach the finish line and complete his part of the race. It's just that easy!

Add this extra time to the winning horse's time of 95.0 s, and obtain 95.43 *s* as the final time of the second-place finisher.

This method was used throughout this book each time a horse whose data were being analyzed did not finish first. It is not a difficult concept to apply, but it may at first seem tricky. The reader should remember this technique was applied as he reads the following analyses and finds reference to *place* or *show* finishes.

CHAPTER 8

Time is nature's way to keep everything from happening at once.
-- John A. Wheeler

Linear Trend Analysis for Two-Year-Olds

The second portion of the data sieve consists in analyzing the trend lines for each 2YO and 3YO passing the initial data sort cut for each age category.

Recall that the Excel application LINEST was used to generate these trend lines and their pertinent related data, ten pieces of total information for each horse.

Of the ten informational items provided by Excel, only three are immediately important and useful; one is provisionally useful. The most useful are the Slope, the Intercept, and R^2. The Standard Error of Estimate, symbolized STEYX by Excel, is also used in LA. Each of these parameters of linear analysis is now explained in detail.

Slope: The slope of a straight line (technically a line segment) is a number indicating how much the line slants upward from left to right or downward from left to right *per unit increase* in horizontal distance.

It is a familiar number to highway construction engineers and simply indicates how steep a hill is, for example. They usually call it the *grade* of the road.

For instance, you've probably seen highway warning signs for trucks indicating a 5-percent downhill grade ahead for perhaps two miles. This means that the highway is dropping in elevation by 5 percent (264 feet) of a mile for each mile traveled horizontally.

Intercept: The intercept of a straight line is the point where it intersects the vertical or y-axis. It shows how far above the x-axis the line is at that point. That's all there is to intercept. It is mainly a marker, as stated previously.

The slope and intercept *uniquely determine* where a straight line falls on a given graph. You will have an example of this after the next table summarizing the 2YO trends is presented.

Coefficient of Determination: As also mentioned earlier, the Coefficient of Determination, COD, is symbolized by R^2. It tells how close the straight line comes to fitting the data it is intended to represent. More will be said shortly about it.

The maximum possible R^2 values are $\pm$ 1.00. Those values imply a perfect mathematical fit of a line to the data. The smallest possible value for R^2 is 0.00. This value indicates a totally random relationship between the data and the straight line. For that case, the line passes horizontally through the midpoint of the scatter of data points. It predicts nothing concerning the change in the dependent variable, y, with respect to x.

Standard Error of Estimate: The Standard Error of Estimate, STEYX, is analogous to the regular standard deviation of sample data discussed previously. The "STE" portion refers to the term "standard error," and the "YX" part refers to predicting Y values (times) from X values (distances) for the given data.

Each of the above four items – Slope, Intercept, COD and STEYX – is listed in Table 7 following. Table 7 summarizes the LTA, for the 2YOs from the preliminary sort.

Table 7

Final Linear Trend Analysis Results for Two-Year-Olds

Horse	LTA Score	LTA Rank	BHI Rank	Slope	Intercept	COD (R²)	STEYX
Landaluce	154	1	NA	108.55	-13.26	0.999	0.260
First Flight	150	2	NA	94.37	-2.15	0.993	0.795
Ruffian	139	3	35	93.87	-1.60	0.997	0.189

Table 7 – continued

Personal Ensign	131	4	48	108.80	-12.40	1.00*	0.00*
Seattle Slew	118	5	9	96.80	-2.50	0.999	0.245
Secretariat	109	6	2	103.44	-7.09	0.996	0.992
Affirmed	108	7	12	103.90	-7.55	0.991	1.467
Sunday Silence	108	7 (tie)	31	118.88	-19.76	0.998	0.297
Alydar	103	8	27	102.68	-6.63	0.995	1.220
Spectacular Bid	98	9	10	99.08	-3.57	0.996	1.188
Nashua	88	10	24	96.23	-1.73	0.982	1.398
Optimistic Gal	79	11	NA	103.54	-6.42	0.983	1.888

*Personal Ensign ran only twice as a 2YO. Therefore, her COD and STEYX values are unrealistic and cannot be used for predictions.

The horses listed in Table 7 represent the ten highest ranked (and tied) 2YOs based on the preliminary sort followed by an LTA. The primary data from the LTA is in the last four columns of Table 7. Excursus F gives the full LTA results for 2YOs.

Excursus F
Complete 2YO LTA Results

LTA Parameters					
Horse	Slope	Intercept	COD (R²)	STEYX	LTA Score
Landaluce	108.55	-13.26	0.9998	0.2602	154
First Flight	94.37	-2.15	0.9928	0.7954	150
Ruffian	93.87	-1.60	0.9974	0.1885	139
Personal Ensign	108.80	-12.40	1.0000	0.0000	131
Seattle Slew	96.80	-2.50	0.9998	0.2449	118
Secretariat	103.44	-7.09	0.9963	0.9925	109

Excursus F – continued

Affirmed	103.90	-7.55	0.9912	1.4664	108
Sunday Silence	118.88	-19.76	0.9976	0.2970	108
Alydar	102.68	-6.63	0.9954	1.2204	103
Spectacular Bid	99.08	-3.57	0.9957	1.1884	98
Nashua	96.23	-1.73	0.9823	1.3978	88
Optimistic Gal	103.54	-6.42	0.9832	1.8883	79
Cutoff for LA*					
Dr. Fager	98.53	-2.81	0.9952	0.9670	67
La Prevoyante	109.38	-10.26	0.9944	1.3673	67
Native Dancer	100.95	-4.18	0.9847	1.7711	63
Count Fleet	103.53	-6.02	0.9926	1.4161	58
Citation	107.70	-8.59	0.9822	2.3231	50
Man o' War	96.04	0.21	0.9745	0.8687	47
Colin	97.01	-0.68	0.9856	0.9529	43
Equipoise	100.95	-3.62	0.9884	2.0900	39
Damascus	96.61	0.39	0.9983	0.3027	29

*Cutoff point for advancing to Limits Analysis

The calculation of the trend line sort points given in column two will be explained shortly.

It would be handy if one could simply use the slopes and intercepts from Table 7 and thereby immediately see why each horse rated its final ranking.

However, the numbers can be somewhat deceiving, and one cannot plot as many trend lines (eleven in this case) as are represented above on one graph for comparison. The lines are simply too close together to visually differentiate when they are graphed simultaneously.

In principle, if one could form a comparison graph as presented in Chart 8 below, there would be little problem with quick visual interpretation and ranking of results.

Chart 8
Multiple Trend Line Example

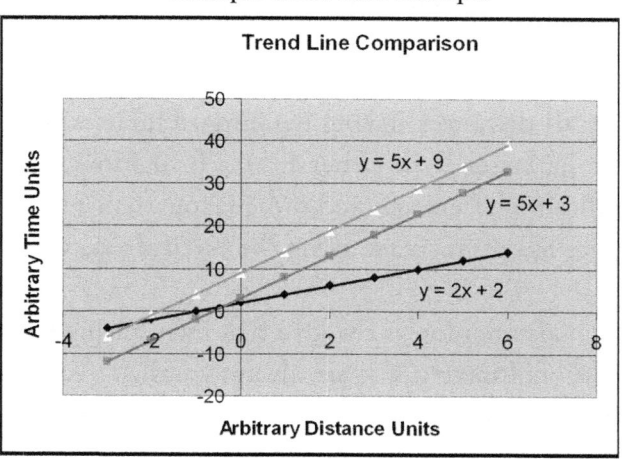

For this generic graph the data were purposely arranged to yield the three lines positioned as shown. The actual equation for each line is included beside it. Other than for this example, all linear trend graphs in this book show distances (in miles) plotted along the horizontal axis and times (in seconds) plotted along the vertical axis.

Ideally, if the trend lines for three horses, say Horse A, Horse B and Horse C were positioned, in that order, from bottom to top of the graph as in Chart 8, then one could immediately tell that Horse A was the fastest of the three for all distances involved.

Distances left of the vertical axis are, of course, not used because they are negative and nonexistent. They are merely a consequence of the mathematical method (least squares) used to generate the trend lines from their respective data by Excel's LINEST routine.

What these lines do clearly show, however, is that Horse A has the fastest times at all distances that are positive or real.

This can be seen from the *slopes and intercepts of these lines, taken in combination.*

In each case, the slope is the number multiplying x. For the bottom line it is 2; for the middle line it is 5, and for the top line it is 5.

The respective intercepts are: bottom line = 2; middle line = 3; top line = 9.

101

Look closely at the vertical axis, the one numbered from -20 at the bottom to 50 at the top, and you will see that the three lines do in fact cross that axis at the numerical points 2, 3 and 9.

Knowing the intercepts and the respective slopes, you can also see that, for all distances having meaning, Horse A will always be predicted to be faster than either Horse B or Horse C. Likewise, Horse B will always be predicted to be faster than Horse C – since running times always increase along the vertical axis with increasing distances.

The graph also reinforces the idea that lines having the same slope – the number multiplying x – are always parallel. You can thus see the mathematics turned directly into a simple geometric picture in this graph.

The above example and chart were presented to show what might make life easy *if* it could be directly applied to the data in this study.

However, with this number of horses and much closer numerical data, the lines do not separate enough on a graph to tell visually which horse is best at all given distances.

Note that a given horse can be faster at some distances and slower at others. This is shown by their trend lines crossing at some point, as Chart 8 would show if negative distances were realistic.

In that case, Horse A *would eventually become slower* than either Horse B or Horse C at those points where his trend line crossed *and then rose higher* on the graph than their respective lines.

Since simple visual inspection could not easily be used for the current data, the times derived from each of the trend lines listed in Table 7 for each horse at a set of eight distances were used to determine the fastest overall horse.

The distances selected for study ranged from 0.500 miles (4 f) to 1.0625 miles (8.5 f) for the 2YOs. They generally represent the distance limits run by any of the 2YO horses.

In all, since 21 horses had calculated times compared at each of eight distances, then 21 x 8 or 168 data points were generated by computer from LINEST for analysis.

The Shapiro-Wilk Normalcy Test

Each set of 21 times for each distance was first checked for normalcy of its parent distribution using the Shapiro-Wilk Test.

All sets proved normal. The Shapiro-Wilk probabilities ranged from 0.13 to 0.92. For this study, a probability of 0.05 or less is required to show possible non-normalcy. Therefore, standard comparison statistics could be used on these data.

The reader should realize that, even when a sample as large as 100 is drawn randomly from a *known normal distribution*, it does not always test as normal. This is shown in chart 9 below.

The Shapiro-Wilk test for the distribution in Chart 9 gave a p-value of 0.6257. This implies that the chance of it coming from a normal distribution was about 62.5 percent. We know, in fact, that it *was from* a normal distribution having mean = 98 and standard deviation = 2, because it was set up that way using Excel!

Even though it was drawn from a known normal distribution, this sample had a kurtosis of 1.017 and a skewness of -0.066. Thus, one cannot categorically say that normal populations guarantee perfectly normal samples!

Chart 9
Randomly Generated Histogram of n = 100; Mean = 97.93,
Standard Deviation = 2.0, Shapiro-Wilk Normalcy Test: p = 0.6257

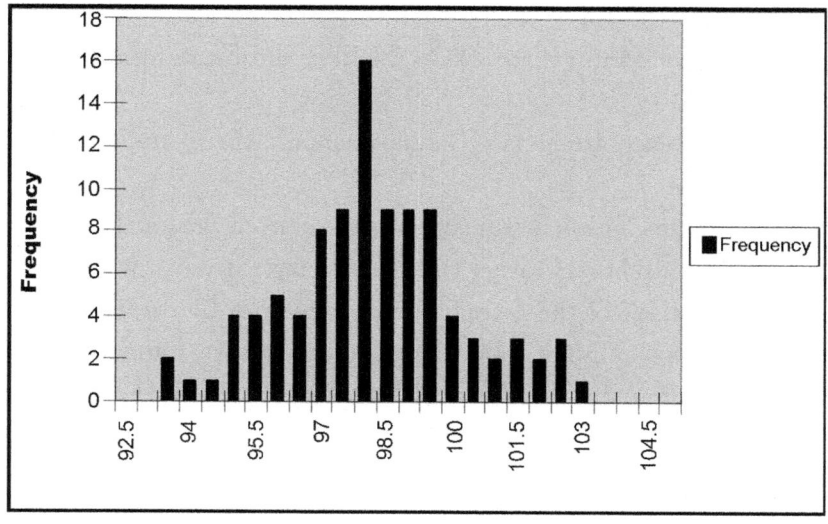

Proceeding with the linear trend results, since 21 points was the maximum score a given horse could earn for each of the eight distances, the maximum possible score for 2YOs was, therefore, 168 points.

The Top Three Two-Year-Olds

The top three 2YO scorers were: Landaluce, First Flight, and Ruffian. Personal Ensign finished fourth but could not advance to LA because her LTA data contained only two data points. Two points always determine a straight line. Therefore, this made her STEYX value automatically zero. The value zero cannot be used in LA analysis.

The reader may now be concerned at the final placement of Man o' War – in eighteenth position and just ahead of three horses.

As is explained in detail in the following chapter, special adjustments were made to Man o' War's data for both his 2YO and 3YO campaigns.

Identical adjustments were made for every horse that ran *before* 1950 and whose data were compared with others in this study. This seemed equitable.

The adjustments mainly involve compensation for the weight of steel shoes Man o' War and other pre-1950 horses wore, as opposed to the aluminum shoes worn by many modern horses. Adjustments for track conditions were also included.

Even after the adjustments, Man o' War's times still did not beat those of the stated top three 2YOs. Neither did Secretariat's for that matter!

Facts, however, are facts. The numbers are there, and there is no denying them.

The numbers and their adjustments are entirely reasonable. In fact, they *aided* certain horses rather than penalizing them in any way.

Based on LTA of the distances and times run by these horses, as documented in the DRFC, and the preliminary sort, Landaluce, First Flight and Ruffian are the top candidates for best 2YO Thoroughbred of the past century. However, there remains the final test, Limits

Analysis, discussed in the chapter after next, before final conclusions can be reached.

As a reminder, a given horse's time for any distance is determined by first multiplying that distance, in miles, by the slope given in column five of Table 7.

The intercept number in column six of Table 7 is then added to the previous result, and the time, in seconds, predicted for that horse and that distance is then given.

This is exactly what was done for all the time values used in this study of the 2YO LTAs and for the previous Secretariat example at 3 f.

Before presenting the results of the LTA for 3YOs and the final LA comparisons for both age groups, a discussion of the shoe or plate corrections and the corrections for track condition, as applied to Man o' War's and other pre-1950 data, is warranted.

CHAPTER 9

So maybe what we call imaginary time is really more basic, and what we call real time is just an idea that we invent to help us describe what the universe is like.
-- Stephen Hawking

Introduction to Data Adjustments

This chapter concerns data adjustments to the records of Man o' War, First Flight and to those of other horses running before 1950. These adjustments are necessary to maintain the spirit of fairness and impartiality desired in this study.

Some Thoroughbred racing fans become irascibly vocal regarding the unfairness of judging Man o' War or other horses of his *era* against more *modern* horses. Their primary arguments focus on the presumed handicaps horses faced years ago.

In fact, a horse like Man o' War needs no excuses for his splendid track record. However, an exploration of the arguments *against* comparing horses of different eras will not hurt, and it may clarify issues.

Seven Era Arguments and Man o' War

According to his advocates, the basic reasons hampering Man o' War from achieving an even greater record generally include:

1. Wearing heavier steel plates (shoes). Modern horses use aluminum plates, and these allow more speed.
2. Running on slower tracks.

3. Starting from the old starting barrier (a spring-loaded net) which did not provide a fair, uniform start.
4. Not being trained as well or as completely.
5. Having lower quality food which did not provide the same energy as do modern foods.
6. Wasting his energy due to the way he ran.
7. Being subjected to comparisons (between himself and modern horses) which are, a priori, axiomatically futile.

It is interesting that the very people saying comparisons are futile are often the ones citing the 1999 BHI ranking as gospel for Man o' War's greatness.

The BHI study itself is based on comparisons founded only on the opinions of seven people, with one of its own panelists (Mr. William Nack) voicing strong reservations about the results.

Discussion of the Arguments

The first three of the above assertions will be discussed sequentially in depth. The remaining items will be given as little comment as deemed necessary to show them spurious or severely lacking in merit.

Argument 1: Steel versus Aluminum Racing Plates

Standard handbooks of Physics and Chemistry supply data on the densities of common substances. The density (often called specific gravity) of a substance is simply its weight per unit volume.

Aluminum is an element containing only traces of impurities. The steels used in many industries, including manufacture of racing plates, are alloys and include various percentages of carbon, chromium, cobalt, magnesium and other elements.

The density of aluminum is listed in standard references as 2.70 grams per cubic centimeter (2.70 gm/cc). The density of one basic grade of all-purpose steel, such as can be used in racing plates, is 7.85 gm/cc.

Dividing 7.85 by 2.70 tells us that racing-plate steel is about 2.91 times heavier, per unit volume, than aluminum. Thus, immediate comparisons are possible between the two types of plates simply by directly weighing one type on an appropriately sensitive scale and then calculating the proportionally higher or lower weight of the other.

Another comparison can be made if the exact volume of a plate is known; the volume can be found by immersing the plate totally in water in a graduated beaker and seeing how far the water rises. A direct reading of plate volume is then possible from the beaker markings since an object displaces its exact volume of liquid when so immersed. The volume is then multiplied by the density to obtain the weight.

This method is handy for those preferring graduated beakers to scales, but it is more roundabout.

The Internet site of Saint Croix Forge was consulted for information on the size and weights of typical plates used for Thoroughbred racing (21).

A mid-range size of 6 was chosen as a fair approximation to the size of shoe that either Secretariat or Man o' War might have worn.

Sizes of the St. Croix plates ranged from 4 through 8.

From the table of weights provided by St. Croix Forge, it was determined that a complete set of four aluminum plates (the front plates were about 5.7 grams per plate heavier than the hind plates) weighed 0.78 lb, after converting from grams per cubic centimeter (gm/cc) to pounds per cubic inch (lb/in^3) and doing the required math.

Therefore, a set of steel plates *exactly* the same size and shape (and, thus, volume) as an aluminum set would weigh 2.9 x 0.78 lb, or 2.26 lb.

At this point an estimate was made that steel plates were about 80 percent as thick as aluminum. This conclusion rests on additional Internet correspondence with an experienced farrier (22).

He estimated that the older steel plates were from five to six oz each and that aluminum shoes were about half as heavy.

Using his estimate meant that a set of four steel plates weighed about 1.5 lb (24 oz). Therefore, using the 1.8 lb that follows from taking steel plates 80 percent as thick as aluminum is entirely reasonable and, in fact, possibly gives a slight edge in change-in-speed calculations to Man o' War or to all pre-1950 horses to which the correction was applied.

At 80 percent the thickness of aluminum plates, the weight of a set of equivalent steel plates would be 0.80 x 2.26 lb, or 1.80 lb.

This estimated 1.80 lb was assigned as an *added weight* to the jockey-and-tack figure given by DFRC on all calculations of momentum, kinetic energy and running times derived from the standard formulas for pre-1950 horses.

A table was then made, using the kinetic energy formula discussed in Chapter 2, to calculate the maximum by which running times for various distances would be affected by steel versus aluminum plates – including the jockey-plus-tack weight Man o' War carried in each race.

Table 8 gives the results.

Table 8
Times subtracted from Man o' War's data to correct for
steel plates at various distances

Distance (mi)	Time (s)*	Distance (mi)	Time (s)
Age 2		Age 3	
0.625	0.24	1.00	0.38
0.625	0.26	1.00	0.41
0.6875	0.28	1.0625	0.39
0.6875	0.29	1.125	0.44
0.75	0.29	1.125	0.45
0.75	0.29	1.1875	0.45
0.75	0.28	1.25	0.52
0.75	0.28	1.25	0.48
0.75	0.29	1.375	0.54
0.75	0.29	1.5	0.64
		1.625	0.64

* All listed times are negative. That is, they are subtracted from the DRFC stated running times.

The first two columns of the final row under Age 2 in Table 8 are intentionally blank because Man o' War ran one less race at age 2 compared to age 3.

You may wonder why identical distances are sometimes paired with slightly different times. This is because the final time correction calculated from the kinetic energy formula depends upon both the weight carried in a given race and the average speed at which it was run.

Both mass (weight) and speed affect the final calculation for kinetic energy differently, because speed is squared but mass is not. This can be seen by working through an example as was done in Chapter 3.

Chart 10 gives a clear visualization of the data in Table 8. It shows that there exists a strong mathematical relationship between the distance Man o' War ran and how much the steel plates affected his times. Remember that this represents the *maximum value* of time difference he can reasonably be assigned.

Maximum values must be assumed because, given all the unique influences present on a given race day, the horse and jockey ran the most efficient race they were then capable of running – given *those factors and circumstances.*

Therefore, it is justifiable to assume that if Man o' War wore aluminum plates 80 years ago, *he would still have generated the same kinetic energy* because his overall racing strategy and tactics, as influenced by his jockey, would have been identical under identical conditions. They would thus be uniquely determined.

The lighter plates theoretically would have let him run fractional seconds faster, for each distance, as indicated in Chart 10.

Chart 10
The effect of steel plates on Man o' War's times

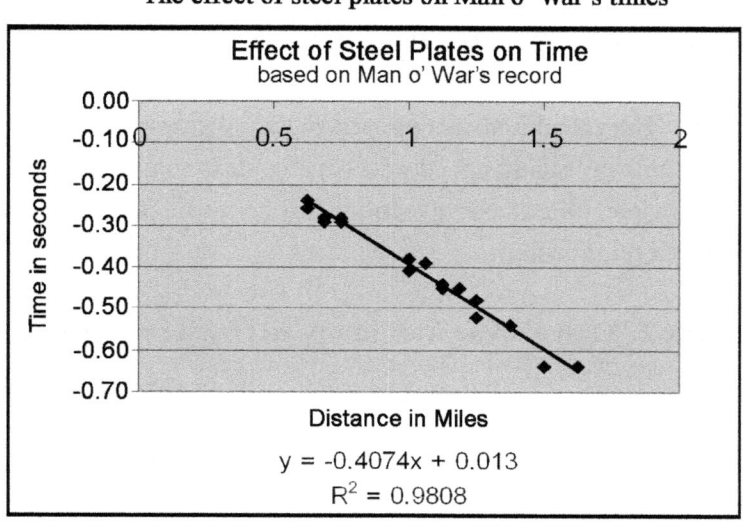

$$y = -0.4074x + 0.013$$
$$R^2 = 0.9808$$

There is no other reasonable conclusion. Any guessing about whether he, in fact, used some other percentage of the energy he *might* have generated is simply that – guessing!

We thus can feel confident that he is being given a fair assessment of how much steel plates affected his speed, and we have achieved a valid compensation for this particular era effect.

By comparison, Tom Ainslie presents an extensive discussion of weight and how it affects the times of races at various distances, based on his racing knowledge (10).

In Chapter 13 on page 226 of his book, Mr. Ainslie offers data indicating that one extra pound of weight slows a horse by one-fifth (0.20) of a second at 10 f (1.25 mi).

A set of steel plates, identical in shape and volume to a set of aluminum plates assumed to be the size worn by Man o' War, are almost exactly *one pound* heavier than the aluminum plates.

Thus, Mr. Ainslie's data indicate that the extra pound of steel plates would have caused Man o' War to run 0.20 seconds slower at 10 f than would aluminum plates.

The present estimate is more liberal. Both Table 8 and Chart 10 credit Man o' War about 0.50 seconds at 10 f. This issue, therefore, appears reasonably settled.

Note, however, the mathematical formula given at the bottom of Chart 10. The high R^2 value, above 0.98, means that the trend line fits the data with at least 98- percent accuracy.

This is not, therefore, some *ad hoc* argument based upon personal preference. The calculated, as opposed to racing-tradition based, effect of plate weight on racing speed and time comes from a time-honored physics principle, kinetic energy, and yields an authentic mathematical equation and relationship.

Argument 2: Man o' War was hampered by slower tracks

Dorothy Ours (23) makes a pertinent statement concerning this point.

On page 58 she explains that both the Saratoga and Belmont tracks were resurfaced during the early twentieth century for the express purpose of making them faster. Saratoga's work was completed in August of 1918, and Belmont's debuted after mid-May 1919.

It so happens that Man o' War ran thirteen of his career 21 races (62%) on one or the other track – and he did not run his first juvenile race until Friday June 6, 1919, well after the surfaces were improved.

Ms. Ours also states that, based on research, numerous records soon fell at both tracks after the improvements and that Belmont even earned the nickname "rubber track" due to its speedy surface.

When one also recalls that Man o' War's records at 1.375 mi (June 1920, Belmont) and 1.625 mi (September 1920 Lawrence Realization, Belmont) held on dirt for 71 and 40 years, respectively (23), one wonders how or why some claim that he was penalized by inferior surfaces.

However, it is possible to address these claims by showing that it was not so much inferior track conditions that made yesteryear's times generally slower as it was the lower competition level.

In fact, **there is no scientific way to measure** the speed of a track on any given day and time and compare it to others on that same day or on previous days.

There is no surface such as the *Standard Thoroughbred Racing Surface*. There is no machine or robot that can travel around a track, measure its resistance in terms applicable to a running horse and then compare the results of races for that day against those run the previous day, week, month, year, decade or century – and adjust accordingly!

Attempts at objective comparison of tracks, such as Beyer Speed Figures or Moss Pace Figures are, in the last analysis, not a major improvement over the Speed Figure and Track Variant discussed earlier in this book, and which were used for sort purposes.

The following charts help weaken the contention that slower tracks significantly hampered Man o' War.

Chart 11
Kentucky Derby Trend Related to Foal Crop Size

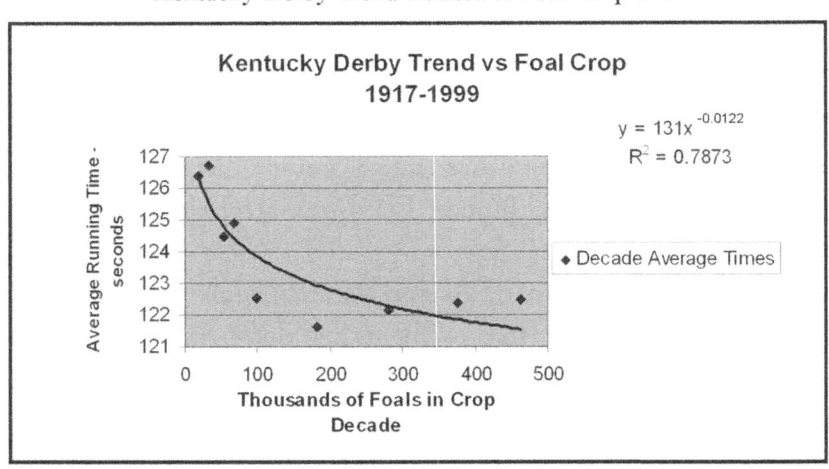

Chart 11 displays nine points, one for each decade from 1910-1919 through 1990-1999.

The *average running time* for the Derby *for each of the nine decades* was plotted versus the average foal crop for that decade, as obtained from the Internet site www.equineonline.com (15).

Rather than present a cumbersome table, the registered foal crop values, *in thousands*, are now listed for each of these nine decades: 1910-19: 18.857; 1920-29: 32.396; 1930-39: 53.368; 1940-49: 68.115; 1950-59: 99.125; 1960-69: 182.533; 1970-79: 280.315; 1980-89: 463.827; 1990-99: 375.291.

The equation of the curve representing foal crop changes, shown in the right margin of the graph, is called a negative power curve. It shows that, as the foal crop size, in x-thousands, increases along the horizontal axis, the average running time for the Kentucky Derby (at 1.25 mi since 1896) drops according to the power -0.0122 of x multiplied by 131.00.

The R^2 value of 0.7873 indicates that the equation fits the data with nearly 79-percent predictive accuracy.

The corresponding power-series trends for the Preakness and Belmont Stakes for the same decades are shown in Charts 12 and 13.

Chart 12
Trend in Preakness Running Times and Foal Crop Size

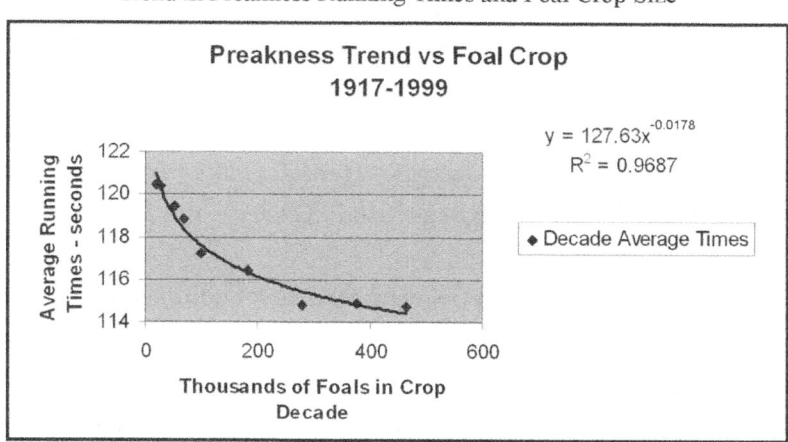

Note that the power curve for the Preakness has parameters of similar magnitude to those of the Kentucky Derby trend. It is relevant that the Coefficient of Determination, R^2, is even higher.

As in Chart 11, the average race time for each decade is plotted versus the size of the North American registered foal crop, in thousands, for that decade.

Chart 13 completes this comparison series. It shows the average Belmont Stakes time trend for the same decades versus the size of foal crop registered.

Chart 13
Trend in Belmont Running Times and Foal Crop Size

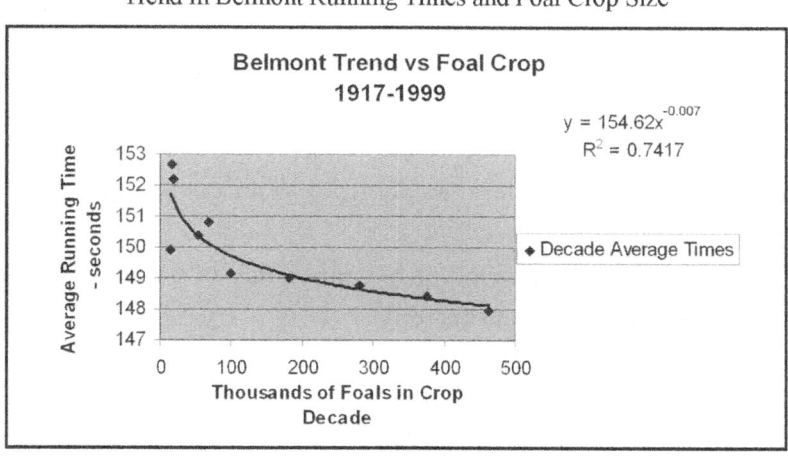

Note again the same general level of fit of equation to data, given by R^2, as held for the two preceding power-series trends.

The average value of R^2 for these three equations, 0.83, representing three entirely different tracks, is not due to chance.

It should be obvious, as will be convincingly suggested by two final related graphs, that *foal crop change is a primary determinant* of how fast a given race will be run across sequential decades – not track condition alone.

One can now intelligently argue that *at least* eighty-three percent of the long-term changes in average running times for the Triple Crown races, and possibly for all G-1 through G-3 level stakes races, are related to the size of the foal crops from which their competitors come.

This means that no more than 17 percent, and possibly less, of the changes in running times over the years since the early twentieth century is attributable to improvements in running surfaces, decreased plate weight or other such factors.

Why should the size of foal crop significantly influence running times? Because the larger the foal crop the greater the genetic diversity represented by worldwide breeding and, therefore, the greater the chances for outstanding runners to be foaled.

Hollingsworth lends a number to this contention. In his words, "Only 59 percent of all Thoroughbreds ever win part of a purse; only 2.5 percent ever win a stakes race. The probability of breeding a stakes winner is scant."(12) Ours (23) puts a 5% level on this figure, and the 487 listed champions of the DRFC (2) represent only 0.03% of all foals from 1890 through 1999 that have won multiple stakes races!

These figures argue strongly that Man o' War, as great as he was for his era, was not so much hampered by track conditions or steel plates as he was able to succeed at least partly from lesser competition. He was genetically ahead of his time.

This fact will offend some of his adherents, but it is undeniable. More will be added later on this topic.

Chart 14 strengthens the argument that the three foal crop trends just presented are not a fluke of chance.

The graph in Chart 14 is a generic plot of the time trend, for the same decades included in the preceding three charts. It shows, however, the *reciprocal* of foal crop size per decade.

Taking the reciprocal (i.e., 1 divided by the size) of the foal crop allows us to plot a generic declining time trend verses increases in foal crop.

The important point is that *this curve is totally independent of* the results of a given race. It is a general plot showing how the inverse of foal crop size tends to decline decade-wise across the entire twentieth century.

In fact, foal crop data *from different years than previously cited,* but for the same decades, was used in generating this plot. This was intentionally done to minimize bias if it was present. Bias seems missing. Foal crop trends definitely mirror and influence performance trends – period.

Chart 14
Inverse Foal Crop Trend: Twentieth Century

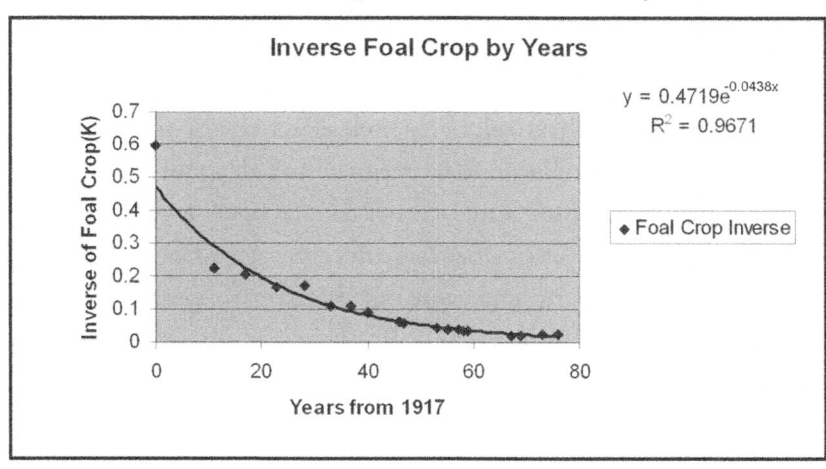

Don't let the equation in the right margin of the graph intimidate you. It is an exponential equation, as identified by the letter *e*. The letter *e* is called the base of natural logarithms, and is easily understood.

The symbol "*e*" represents a number, 2.718 to three decimal places, just as pi represents the number 3.14. The letter "*x*" in the equation indicates how many years after 1917, the first data point, you wish to calculate the inverse of the foal crop size.

If you want the year 1940, for example, x is 23, because 1940 is 23 years after 1917.

Some hand-held calculators directly display *e* to a negative power, as it is in the above equation. This is a handy feature.

Once *e* to the power of the negative value of *x* is obtained, it is multiplied by the coefficient 0.4719, and that gives the value of the *inverse foal crop* for the year 1940. When the reciprocal of that inverse is then calculated, the estimate of how many *thousands* of foals were born in 1940 is determined. In this case, $\hat{y}$ is 0.172 and the inverse of $\hat{y}$ is $(1 / 0.172)$ K = 5.803 K. This predicted value differs by only 3.1% from the actual value of registered North American foals for the year 1940 – 6,003 (15).

For several years in the late 1960s, Canadian foal crop numbers were combined with American foal crop numbers and reported thus by many sources, possibly including the one used herein.

However, since The American Racing Manual 2005 (8) lists Canadian foal crops at around 2500 for the years 1993, 2002 and 2003, it may be assumed they were smaller for the dates concerned in the above charts. Therefore, they would have relatively little effect on the conclusions.

Technically, Puerto Rican foals are included also, but these are only about 600 per year. Since American races are open to Canadian and Puerto Rican horses, all this does not affect the statistical conclusions.

Note that the generic equation fits the data to nearly 97 percent accuracy, as indicated by the value of R^2. Thus the answer just obtained is within the margin of error for the equation.

The preceding is an explanation of what the equation means and how it is used. You should not be concerned further about it, but should realize that it is an accurate representation or model of the published foal crop data.

The fact that the equation in Chart 14 is related to a set of equations which predict changes in running times for three major races across nine decades of the twentieth century with at least 83-percent accuracy is impressive.

These tracks range from Churchill Downs in Louisville, Kentucky to Pimlico in Baltimore, Maryland to Belmont at Elmont, New York.

Let us, however, add one further piece of evidence, if for no other reason than to give the West Coast equal time.

The Santa Anita Derby began in 1935. It is a 9 f, G-1 stakes race for 3YOs. When the average decade running times for this race are plotted versus foal crop, another curve is generated which fits the data with nearly 93 percent accuracy, as Chart 15 shows.

Chart 15
Santa Anita Derby Running Times and Foal Crop Size

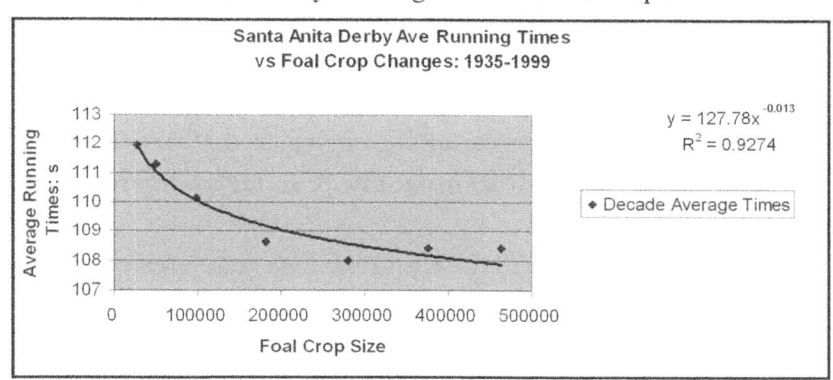

The case should now be sufficiently strong that foal crop probably determines more regarding how horses from different eras compare than does track surface alone.

However, a final fact about these trends needs mentioning. The foal crops between the two final decades represented by the foregoing charts actually *reversed* direction during those two decades. This trend is both informative and critical.

That is, the foal crop for 1980-1989 was 463,827, whereas that for 1990-1999 was 375,291. These numbers represent a slight upward trend for the inverse, not clearly visible in Chart 14, in the tail of the graph.

Significantly, a slight increase is *also shown* in running times for the three separate graphs for the Kentucky Derby, Preakness and Belmont for the final two decades. The Santa Anita average remains constant.

Thus, the average running time for those races actually increases in step with the corresponding decline in foal crop, or at least remains constant.

Enough has now been said to indicate convincingly that foal crop significantly affects running times, and we proceed to the next argument against comparing horses from different eras.

Argument 3: The Net Starting Barrier was Unfair

The most efficient way to dispel this accusation is to review some comments on the issue by Marshall (Mars) Cassidy, as quoted in Ours (23). Mr. Cassidy was an experienced, well-known and respected starter of many years at the time Man o' War raced.

On page 61 Cassidy is quoted as telling Louis Feustel, Man o' War's trainer, that Man o' War broke so far out [when the barrier lifted for his maiden race] that for a brief instant he [Cassidy] nearly recalled the horses!

For an article appearing in the *New York Times* on Sunday December 2, 1923 Mr. Cassidy commented [referring to the newly considered electro-mechanical starting gates] that there was *no machine he could imagine that could properly handle excited horses* [italics mine] as well as a man on the track. And further, such horses would not stand in a box-like contrivance any more than they would stand still on an open track. (See reference note on page 298 for actual quote.)

Pre-race troubles caused by distressed horses in mechanical starting gates are also sensitively documented by Lawrence Scanlan in his recent book (24).

Regarding horses losing time at the barrier, it is also mentioned that jockeys who had become accustomed to Mr. Cassidy's starting technique knew that he often bent his knee slightly just before pressing the barrier's release button, held behind him, and that they anticipated this to gain a quick start. (See Note 7, page 298)

To conclude remarks on this argument, it should be apparent to even the casual observer of television racing that many horses are extremely agitated by the modern starting gates (as Mr. Cassidy's prescience foresaw) and obviously waste energy fighting them in addition to endangering themselves and their riders.

One need only recall the tragic start of the 2006 Preakness in which Barbaro charged through the gate in anticipation of the starting bell. In so doing, he probably injured himself enough that, when the race was restarted, he could not place his weight normally and thus fractured bones -- eventually leading to his death.

It is unreasonable to assume, based on even the short commentary above, that Man o' War was significantly slowed regarding his starts and that the barrier affected his running times unduly. After all, he lost only once!

It is highly likely that modern starting gates do as much harm as good and that they do not significantly enhance quick starts and faster or more reliable times.

There is no practical way to study this phenomenon scientifically due to the resources and logistics required. Thus, most talk on this matter is pure conjecture and opinion. However, common sense is always a good alternate!

Argument 4: Training was Inferior

Again, quoting Ours (23), there is every indication that Louis Feustel, Man o' War's trainer, was highly qualified and put his horse through paced training routines much as current trainers would.

For instance, during his sophomore season, Man o' War beat Wildair three times. The distances were from 8 f to 9 f. Wildair was trained by James G. Rowe, Sr., one of the acknowledged outstanding trainers of all time. To recite his accomplishments would consume too much space and not add significantly to this argument.

Therefore, the comparatively young Lou Feustel proved himself early in his career. Accusations of inferior training are unsubstantiated and dubious, at best.

Argument 5: Food was of Lower Quality

Oats are oats! And although additional nutrients are used, oats were and still are an essential fare of Thoroughbreds. Since there is not much substance to this argument and it certainly has not been, and possibly cannot be, scientifically studied, little more need be added.

If anything, methods of farming and generating produce in the early twentieth century likely yielded foods with higher nutritional value than those currently available.

One equine nutritional expert agreed to allow quoting him in this regard. According to Mr. Don Kapper, "It is *highly likely* that Thoroughbreds from the early twentieth century consumed foods equivalent to or even better in balanced nutrients than did horses later in the century due mainly to the amount of and better balanced nutrients found in the ingredients then, versus what we have analyzed and are feeding horses today. This is due to a change in the genetics of the plants and fertilization practices of the soils where they are grown and the methods of crop treatment."(25)

One only need ask whether Man o' War could have maintained the weight he did – he was a large, muscular Thoroughbred of nearly 1,200 pounds as a three-year-old – or set the records he held for so long on a nutrition-poor diet. Look at his photographs; use common sense; judge accordingly.

Argument 6: Man o' War Wasted Energy

Once again, Ours provides contradictory evidence.

On page 62 she remarks that most racehorses stretched out long and low. However, Man o' War's tendency was to spring up and onward similar to a boulder from a catapult – similar, in fact, to a well-known move by Secretariat (documented on film) when he finally got bored and decided it was time to pass the field!

Man o' War had a high knee action which could look like wasted energy but was, in fact, a *"seamless phase of this powerful arc."* (23)

To the contrary, human athletes often squander *their talents* and, subsequently, their energies. Humans have a perversity in this regard that horses do not.

Man o' War ran as he was genetically inclined to run. He had no hidden agendas and did not engage in the equivalent of thinking, *My* contract is not as good as it should be so therefore I'm not going to try my best today. Screw these guys!

Horses generally give their all, unless they are so beset by the ingratitude and ineptness of owners, trainers and jockeys that they become dispirited – as witness Seabiscuit's lackluster performances before coming under the ownership of Charles Howard. (26)

Man o' War was handled with human kindness, solicitude and affection throughout his life. Ms. Ours text makes this abundantly clear.

A famous photograph on the September 13, 1941 cover of Saturday Evening Post drives this point home – with big rivets. All who love Thoroughbreds should take a long look at it. It shows Big Red and his groom, Will Harbut, sharing one of the more poignant relationships imaginable.

Man o' War did not need to sulk and waste energy in any manner, and he did not. He was sometimes temperamental, but he went all out, as far as his jockey would allow, on the track.

He was one of the greatest Thoroughbreds of all time, and his records prove it. Certainly records are made to be broken and do eventually fall. That is partly due to a newcomer having something to strive for. It could, for example, be debated whether any given human athlete would have been as good as they became without first having an established record to strive toward.

Man o' War, in his time, was his own point of reference, as was Secretariat for his.

Argument 7: Axiomatically Futile Comparisons

If ever a dogmatic assertion was uttered, this is it!

Many people categorically state that one cannot compare horses, or any athletes for that matter, from different eras.

Of course one can compare. The question is whether such comparisons are unbiased and whether they prove anything.

The z-score, at minimum, is one way to make valid and unbiased "era" comparisons. It is discussed later.

This book would not exist if I believed that valid, unbiased comparisons were, a priori, impossible. The remainder of this book will stand as an extended example of how I answered this argument. The reader may judge the success or failure of the attempt.

Whether such judgment is positive or negative does not prove that era comparisons are invalid. It may mean that the comparisons herein were found significantly lacking, but it still does not support a basically defensive statement intended to squelch all thoughts contrary to the beliefs of the person uttering it.

That stated, we are now prepared to discuss the results of the LTA for 3YOs in the following chapter, minus the discarded baggage of at least seven needless distractions.

CHAPTER 10

Time is clothed in different garments for each role it plays in our thinking.
-- John A. Wheeler

Linear Trend Analysis for the Three-Year-Olds

The linear trend analysis results for the 3YOs were done using the same protocol as for the 2YOs.

Therefore, this interpretative chapter is much shorter than was Chapter 8.

Table 9 presents the top ten 3YOs according to their LTAs. Excursus G also shows the horses below the cutoff that did not advance to Limits Analysis.

Excursus G
Complete Results of 3YO Trend Analysis

Horse	Slope	Intercept	COD (R²)	STEYX	LTA Score
Secretariat	102.67	-7.92	0.9944	1.8818	199
Alydar	103.97	-8.99	0.9973	0.9033	182
Dr. Fager	104.79	-9.87	0.9967	0.8775	178
Ruffian	105.19	-10.33	0.9996	0.6676	175
Cigar	99.12	-3.45	0.9959	0.9973	173
Easy Goer	106.34	-11.51	0.9906	2.0285	165
Affirmed	106.40	-11.54	0.9973	1.1363	154

Excursus G – continued

Seattle Slew	109.97	-15.62	0.9984	0.9036	151
Spectacular Bid	107.03	-12.16	0.9978	0.9431	147
Kelso	104.00	-8.49	0.9995	0.9787	137
Cutoff for LA					
Round Table	101.44	-4.95	0.9667	2.5762	124
Bold Ruler	105.28	-9.71	0.9964	1.1711	116
Buckpasser	110.17	-15.11	0.9988	1.2802	114
Man o' War	98.47	-1.18	0.9926	1.8134	106
Skip Away	100.79	-3.81	0.9567	2.7122	99
Optimistic Gal	102.34	-5.52	0.9947	1.6140	91
Personal Ensign	110.32	-13.66	0.9996	0.4180	64
Count Fleet	103.05	-5.67	0.9967	1.2284	62
Citation	104.35	-6.90	0.9969	1.8878	54
War Admiral	102.89	-4.44	0.9978	1.1254	35
First Flight	108.39	-10.19	0.9991	0.4664	31
La Prevoyante	117.31	-18.16	0.9949	1.7661	26

Table 9
Final Linear Trend Analysis Results for Top Three-Year-Olds

Horse	LTA Points	Sort Rank	BHI Rank	Slope	Intercept	R^2	STEYX
Secretariat	199	1	2	102.67	-7.92	0.9944	1.8817
Alydar	182	2	27	103.97	-8.98	0.9972	0.9032
Dr. Fager	178	4	6	104.78	-9.86	0.9967	0.8774
Ruffian	175	6	35	105.19	-10.33	0.9996	0.6675
Cigar	173	3	18	99.12	-3.45	0.9958	0.9973
Easy Goer	165	8	34	106.34	-11.51	0.9906	2.0285
Affirmed	154	5	12	106.40	-11.54	0.9973	1.1363
Seattle Slew	151	7	9	109.97	-15.62	0.9984	0.9036
Spectacular Bid	147	9	10	107.02	-12.15	0.9977	0.9431
Kelso	137	10	4	104.00	-8.49	0.9995	0.9787

As for the 2YOs, the LTA Points in column two of Table 9 were gained by awarding twenty-two points for the fastest time at each distance, twenty-one points for the second fastest time, and so forth down to one point for the slowest predicted time.

This point award system was based on there being twenty-two 3YO horses in the LTA pool.

Ten distances were involved for the 3YOs, as opposed to eight for the 2YOs. These distances ranged from 6 f (0.75 mi) to 13 f (1.625 mi).

The highest attainable point score was, therefore, 220. Obtaining that score would have required a given horse to have the shortest predicted time for each of the ten distances. The distances were selected as typical for this age group to run.

Secretariat's top score of 199 thus shows that he dominated most of the 3YO speed-for-distance categories.

For direct comparison purposes, remember that Table 9 represents information equivalent to that of Table 7 for 2YOs in Chapter 8.

The next chapter describes the results of analyzing the three-sigma limits (also called Limits Analysis or LA) for each of the ten horses advancing from the LTA for both the 2YOs and 3YOs.

The horse(s) having the highest combined LTA and LA points will be the candidate greatest horse(s) of the twentieth century.

At that point, little can be added from a statistical standpoint. Readers may agree or disagree with the results. Such would be expected in any study like this.

Considering the small samples involved, it is extremely fortunate – serendipitous might be the better descriptor – that the linear trends fit the data with such high accuracy and that the majority of the run time samples were normally distributed.

Had these conditions not been met, one might as well have resorted to personal opinion – the arbitrariness of which prompted this study originally!

Chapter 11 presents the results of the Limits Analysis for both the 2YOs and 3YOs that advanced from the LTAs with the highest scores.

CHAPTER 11

Time will run back and fetch the age of gold.
-- John Milton

Limits Analysis for the Two- and Three-Year-Olds

This chapter presents the final level of data analysis for the 2YO and 3YO champions selected from both the BHI rankings and the six additional horses.

The type of analyses presented herein may be termed either *Three-Sigma Analysis* (TSA) or *Limits Analysis* (LA). Both terms are equally descriptive. Since it is shorter, the term "LA" will be used henceforth.

To clarify terms before proceeding, statisticians commonly call one standard deviation *"one sigma"* because a lower-case Greek letter σ (sigma) is used to denote the population standard deviation.

Hence, the term *three-sigma* simply means the range of sample values between ±3 SD on either side of the sample mean.

In Thoroughbred racing negative or minus 3 sigma (-3 σ) denotes the shortest likely time for a given horse to run a given race, whereas positive or plus 3 sigma (+3 σ) indicates the slowest likely time.

If we know that a sample of the times it takes a horse to run a given distance is normally or near normally distributed, then that time distribution may be simultaneously compared to other similar distributions in a special and highly convenient way using the 3-sigma limits.

Such comparison directly tells us the percent of times a given horse is likely either to have won or lost to another horse, had they raced a large number of times, say 100.

It *cannot tell which horse will win a given race*, but it can tell the average number of likely wins if multiple races were run. It is, therefore, an excellent way to compare quality among Thoroughbreds.

The resulting comparison is, therefore, similar to the *half-life* concept in physics. The half-life of a radioactive substance indicates exactly how long it will take for one-half of the atoms in a particular sample to decay. It does not, however, tell anything about whether a certain atom will be one of those that decay in the stated time interval.

Returning to Thoroughbred racing, normal distributions have a built-in predictive property which has not been fully, or perhaps even marginally, exploited by Thoroughbred data analysts.

The reason normal distributions may be specially compared is that equal *percentages of area* fall under the curve between corresponding standard deviation values within such distributions, as explained previously.

For instance, it was noted that about 68 percent of the area under a normal distribution falls within $\pm 1\ \sigma$ on *either side* of the mean.

One standard deviation below the mean ($-1\ \sigma$) is considered negative and vice versa for $1\ \sigma$ above the mean. In racing, negative sigmas are good. They denote faster than average times.

For practical purposes, all the times from a normal sample of racing data fall within $\pm 3\ \sigma$ on either side of the mean, i.e., within the 3-sigma limits.

Technically, 99.73 percent of the sample values (times a horse runs a given distance) fall within these limits, but any inaccuracy due to ignoring the remaining 0.27 percent will absolutely not affect the results of these analyses.

Chart 16 shows two normal distributions compared on the same horizontal axis.

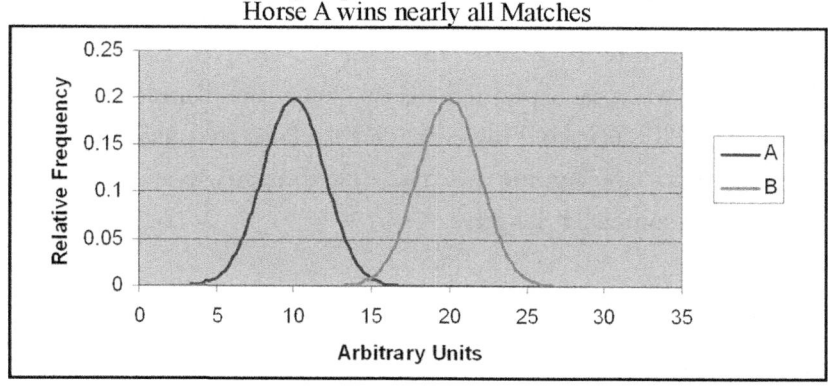

Chart 16
Two Nearly Separated Normal Distributions
Horse A wins nearly all Matches

If these two normal distributions represented the spread in running times for horses A & B at a given distance, we would immediately see that Horse A, having the left-most distribution, would nearly always win, for practical purposes.

This is because most of the time values along the horizontal axis under the distribution representing Horse A are **less than** the corresponding time values for Horse B's distribution.

Of course in this case the values along the horizontal axis are not actual running times. They are merely used for illustration.

However, the principle is exactly the same when running times are substituted, as will be shown.

Therefore, *if we know the mean and standard deviation* of the running-time distributions for two or more horses at a given distance, and also that those distributions are normal or near normal, as verified by the Shapiro-Wilk Test, we can directly compare the distributions and determine what percent of time one horse would win, or lose, compared with the others if they had a series of match races!

To repeat, a single race's result cannot be predicted. If that were possible, many millionaires would be briefly running around race tracks – until all the tracks closed!

This example presents an obvious comparison because the two distributions were essentially separated, at least enough that the comparisons were not significantly affected.

Random Number Generator

For typical cases the distributions overlap more, and further explanation on how to handle the data is required. Excel does the equivalent of what is explained below when the Random Number Generator (RNG) is used. However, it is beneficial to consider manually comparing two overlapping normal distributions even though the explanation is somewhat lengthy.

Chart 17
Two Partly Overlapped Normal Distributions
Used to Explain Basis of Limits Analysis

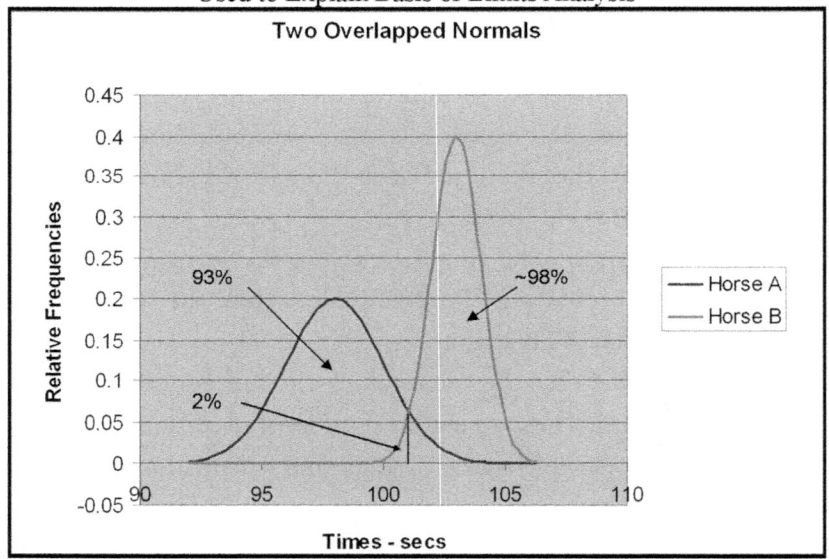

To perform a 3-sigma analysis, remember that the *total area* under each normal curve represents the *total number of races* that each horse might run against another.

It is easiest to let the total area represent 100 units and to equate each hypothetical race between horses to 1 unit of area under each curve.

Do not allow the different heights of the two distributions to give the impression that the higher curve is more important.

The heights are purely relative. In these cases, curve height depends on the width of the curve's base. Excel plots normal distributions so that the total area under the curve remains constant.

Therefore, if one curve's base is half as wide as another's - meaning its standard deviation is narrower - it must be twice as high to contain the same area.

NORMDIST Function

Excel's NORMDIST function is used to manually calculate the percent of area falling *to the left* of a given point along the x-axis (running times) of either curve.

For simplicity, refer all calculations to the point where curves A and B intersect. This point's numerical value is displayed on the computer monitor by Excel when it is touched on screen by the mouse cursor.

In Chart 17, the value of the intersection point is 101. That is, curves A and B intersect at the point representing a time value of 101 seconds.

Use Excel's NORMDIST function to find the area under each curve to the left of this point. Excel provides automatic help on using the NORMDIST function. Basically, one just enters '=NORMDIST(value at desired point, mean of distribution, standard deviation of distribution, true)' into a chosen spreadsheet cell. When the Enter key is pressed the answer then appears.

For this example, 2% of the curve representing Horse B is left of 101 and 93% of the curve for Horse A is left of 101. By subtraction, this means that 98% of the curve for B must be above (to the right of) 101 while 7% of the curve for A is above 101.

One can visually see that Horse A will win most of the hypothetical races simply because A's distribution is so far to the left of B's. Remember that values below (left of) 101 mean faster times.

Therefore, at least 93% of A's times will be faster than all but 2% of B's. This follows logically since the mean of A's distribution is 98 and its standard deviation is 2.00, whereas the mean of B's distribution is 103 and its standard deviation is 1.00.

Horse B's average time is thus 5 seconds slower than A's for the same distance.

It is adequate to assume that each horse wins half the races represented by the two mutually overlapped areas under their respective distributions and on either side of the common intersection point, 101 seconds.

Refer again to Excursus E, if needed, to review how the outcome of a given race for any horse is determined by multiple random factors. This being so, shared portions of areas under normal distributions represent races that, over the long run, will be evenly split (approximately) by the horses just by the nature of randomness acting on their running ability and the times they posted.

Therefore, Horse A and Horse B each win 1 unit (race) in the 2% overlap region. In the 7% overlap region each horse technically wins 3.5 units (races). Since a half race is impossible, it will not matter at this point to award one race more to one horse and call it a 4-3 split in this area.

The totals for all the above calculations resolve to $92 + 3 = 95$ wins for A and the remainder, 5, for B.

All 100 races that either horse could run against the other have thus been accounted for using the normal distribution comparison or Limits Analysis method.

To lend credence to the above example, Excel's RNG was run for both horses, using each horse's particular mean and standard deviation, as stated above, to generate 100 hypothetical races from corresponding normal distributions.

The logic command "=if(A2>C2,1,0)" was then used to compare the results of the 100 simulations. In this case Horse A's running times were placed in cells A2 thru A101 and those of Horse B were placed in C2 thru C101.

The RNG automatically compared the 100 separate values. Its output was 1 if Horse A's time was greater (longer than) Horse B's and was 0 if the opposite held.

The above manually-scored example predicted that Horse A would win about 95 of the 100 races. Two simulations with the RNG yielded 97 and 99. Thus, we were close enough for all practical purposes to show that the 3-sigma method works!

In summary, Horse A is predicted to win at least 95 of 100 races from Horse B, given the normal parameters chosen for this example.

All this information follows precisely from the nature and shape of their distributions – *provided these distributions are normal or near normal.*

The Shapiro-Wilk Test will determine beforehand whether two distributions are normal before they are compared using the above method. One cannot compare obviously non-normal distributions using this method.

❧

The procedure described above was used to compare the top 2YO and 3YO horses from the LTA rankings.

The 2YOs were compared at distances of 6 f, 8 f and 8.5 f. The 3YOs were compared at 7 f, 9 f and 10 f.

These distances were chosen because they were most representative of distances run at the respective ages of two and three by most horses, according to their DRFC records.

In fact, 10 f is a criterion distance for 3YOs in that, unless a horse runs at least one race at that distance, he or she cannot, in principle, win the Triple Crown.

For the present cases, all linear trends fit the data which such exceptional accuracy that slight error would be expected even when two horses were compared at distances they never ran in actual competition.

The average CODs or R^2 values for all 2YOs and 3YOs were 0.9914 and 0.9936, respectively. This means that the respective linear trends predict changes in running times for increasing distance with average accuracies of 99.14 and 99.36 percent, respectively.

One special case needs mention. Personal Ensign only ran twice as a 2YO. Therefore, her LTA value for STEYX, the standard error of the mean, was automatically 0.00. It could not be anything else because two points, no matter what level they are related, always determine a straight line. This is indicated by having zero standard error of the mean.

Since such a number is meaningless and cannot be used for comparisons with other horses, Personal Ensign could not be included in the Limits Analysis. She therefore could not be considered as a candidate greatest horse at age 2.

Limits Analysis Results: Two-Year-Olds

When the top 2YOs were compared using LA for the three distances of 6 f, 8 f and 8.5 f, the final ranking order of the top three horses was as presented in Table 10.

Table 10
Limits Analysis Results for Two-Year-Olds
Number of simulated Races Won Shown in each Column

Horse	6f	8f	8.5f	Total
First Flight	28	85	43	156
Ruffian	0	5	52	57
Landaluce	51	0	0	51
Nashua	5	8	5	18
Affirmed	8	0	0	8
Alydar	3	1	0	4
Optimistic Gal	4	0	0	4
Seattle Slew	0	1	0	1
Spectacular Bid	1	0	0	1
Sunday Silence	0	0	0	0
Secretariat	0	0	0	0
GRAND TOTAL	100	100	100	300

The total points in column five of Table 10 were determined simply by adding the point totals for a given horse at each of the three match distances chosen for the 2YOs.

At each distance, each of the compared horses had its mean and STEYX values entered into the Excel RNG program. Excel then automatically generated 100 possible times for the given distance for each of the horses. In all, 1,100 total random simulations were generated.

For each of the 100 separate simulations, the minimum time value was determined, and the horse having that minimum simulated time was awarded 1 point.

If a single horse had scored the lowest time for all 100 random simulations, it would have received 100 points for that distance.

Therefore, 300 total points were possible for the total three distances simulated.

When all random simulations were completed, the top three 2YO horses, as shown in Table 10, were First Flight, Landaluce and Ruffian, in alphabetic order.

The single most perplexing fact to emerge from these data is that neither First Flight nor Landaluce were selected by the BHI panel as among the top 100 horses of the twentieth century, even though they are listed in the DRFC book.

However, these data certainly show them to be among the top 2YOs.

Perhaps since so many years had elapsed in First Flight's case and the fact that her 3YO season was not remarkable, the BHI panel tended to regard her with less interest.

In Landaluce's case, she unfortunately died within a month after her last race as a 2YO and her career ended summarily with no chance to show further development.

One would have to rate these two fillies at least equivalent as 2YOs to the great Ruffian, even though they are apparently forgotten by racing pundits.

Limits Analysis Results: Three-Year-Olds

The 3YOs were scored on Limits Analysis exactly as were the 2YOs except that their distances were 7 f, 9 f and 10 f.

Table 11 summarizes their points. The top three 3YO rankings went to Secretariat, Easy Goer and Cigar. However, Seattle Slew was just one point below Cigar and, statistical estimates being just that, it is only fair to judge these latter two as being equivalent.

Table 11, in fact, seems to give a much more considered and balanced estimation of the quality of these ten horses than did the BHI ranking.

Even though Man o' War's times, both as a 2YO and as a 3YO were adjusted for plate weights and track conditions, his numbers still did not match those of the top finishers in the Limits Analysis.

It is also noteworthy that Ruffian was the only filly at age three to rank well within the top 10 (#7) on Limits Analysis in this study.

This ranking will later be shown to be highly realistic when the unfinished match race between Ruffian and Foolish Pleasure is simulated 100 times.

Table 11

Limits Analysis Results for Three-Year-Olds

Number of Simulated Races Won Shown in each Column

Horse	7f	9f	10f	Total
Secretariat	16	37	35	88
Easy Goer	20	17	12	49
Cigar	0	11	25	36
Seattle Slew	30	5	0	35
Affirmed	13	9	7	29
Spectacular Bid	10	6	3	19
Ruffian	4	6	7	17
Alydar	3	6	5	14
Dr. Fager	4	2	3	9
Kelso	0	1	3	4
GRAND TOTAL	100	100	100	300

It remains to total the point values for the LTA and LA analyses and to select the candidate greatest horse(s) from each of the 2YO and 3YO categories. That is the task of the following chapter.

CHAPTER 12

In fact, time, the ever-rolling stream, has no more to do with the existence of clocks than with that of sausages.
-- Herbert Dingle

Linear Trend and Limits Analysis Results

This chapter discusses the results of the LTA and the LA for both the 2YOs and 3YOs.

The following chapter presents a series of hypothetical match races between pairs of famous Thoroughbreds.

Five of these pairs of horses actually raced against each other during their careers. One of the matches pits Secretariat against Man o' War, a race which obviously did not occur in real life but which holds tremendous fascination at least as a hypothetical exercise.

For the match races, LA is used to predict which horse from each pair will win the most matches of 100 using Excel's RNG.

Selecting the Top 2YOs

Table 12 summarizes the top horses in each of the two primary age categories of this study. The sum of points for the LTA and the LA is considered the final score for each horse in determining its candidate status as greatest 2YO or 3YO horse.

Table 12

Final Scoring for the 2YOs and 3YOs

Two-Year-Olds					Three-Year-Olds				
Horse	LTA	LA	Total	Rank	Horse	LTA	LA	Total	Rank
First Flight	150	156	306	1	Secretariat	199	88	287	1
Landaluce	154	51	205	2	Easy Goer	165	49	214	2
Ruffian	139	57	196	3	Cigar	173	36	209	3
Seattle Slew	118	1	119	4	Alydar	182	14	196	4
Affirmed	108	8	116	5	Ruffian	175	17	192	5
Secretariat	109	0	109	6	Dr. Fager	178	9	187	6
Sunday Silence	108	0	108	7	Seattle Slew	151	35	186	7
Alydar	103	4	107	8	Affirmed	154	29	183	8
Nashua	88	18	106	9	Spectacular Bid	147	19	166	9
Spectacular Bid	98	1	99	10	Kelso	137	4	141	10
Optimistic Gal	79	4	83	11	**				
Personal Ensign	131	0*	131	*	**				

*Personal Ensign raced only twice as 2YO. She had insufficient data with which to apply Limits Analysis.

**Intentionally blank

As the table notes, Personal Ensign raced only twice as a 2YO. This does not provide enough data on which to run a Shapiro-Wilk test to determine the normalcy of her distribution of running times (minimum three required).

Therefore, she could not honestly be compared to the other 2YO horses via Limits Analysis and was not assigned points in the LA category. It was felt this was the only unbiased way to handle her data.

Personal Ensign, in effect, was thus eliminated from full consideration as candidate greatest 2YO.

Some will object to this situation, but it cannot be helped. The data are simply insufficient in this case, and disagreement will always occur no matter how data are analyzed or handled.

Based on the combined LTA and LA results, the order of finish for the 2YOs was as shown. First Flight finished first with 306 combined LTA and LA points. Landaluce was second with 205 combined points, and Ruffian was a close third with 196 combined points.

A somewhat detailed explanation must now follow because many, if not all, readers will be totally unfamiliar with either First Flight or Landaluce.

That is unfortunate because both were great champions. They are both, in fact, listed in the DRFC book, but neither was picked as a top-100 horse of the twentieth century by the BHI voting panel.

Perhaps the above is true because Landaluce died the month after the final race of her juvenile season, and First Flight's final three years did not match the luster of her juvenile campaign.

First Flight won five of six as a juvenile, two of six as a sophomore and four of twelve as a 4YO. Her overall career record was 11-3-3 out of twenty-four races.

The totals given in Table 12 result from First Flight being given a -0.74 s credit on each of her times for her juvenile year.

This deduction was tentatively granted because she raced in 1946, and an attempt was made to compensate her for the extra weight of steel shoes plus possibly inferior track conditions compared with more recent times. The same basic compensation was given the other pre-1950 horses.

The time compensations were for a combination of extra plate weight due to steel plates and track conditions after estimated foal crop effects were deducted.

However, although the previous foal crop influences on running times show an average 83 percent fit to the data, they apply specifically for the Belmont run at 12 f. First Flight's juvenile races were all at Belmont, but they ranged in distance from 4.5 f to 6.5 f, and cannot be accurately compared with the original Belmont trend line.

Special Comparison: Ruffian and First Flight

It is important to treat each horse's data equally and without prejudice. Therefore, a second extended set of comparisons with Ruffian's times was made using three distinct time values for First Flight.

Table 13 following compares Ruffian's times for the seven LTA distances with three sets of times for First Flight, depending on the amount of time compensation (amount of time subtracted from each of First Flight's 2YO times) she was granted.

Table 13

Comparison of Ruffian's Times with Changes in Time Compensation Δ for First Flight

Horse	Time Δ	Distances in Furlongs – Times Beneath						
		5	5.5	6	6.5	7	8	8.5
Ruffian	none	57.06	62.93	68.80	74.66	80.53	92.26	98.13
First Flight	-0.74s	56.83	62.73	68.62	74.52	80.42	92.22	98.11
First Flight	-0.54s	57.03	62.93	68.28	74.72	80.62	92.42	98.31
First Flight	Varies*	57.32	63.20	69.08	74.96	80.84	92.60	98.48

*Time compensations vary slightly with distance for aluminum racing plate calculations – from -0.23s to -0.30s

The time adjustments were: -0.74 s, -0.54 s, and from -0.23 s to -0.30 s, depending on the length of the race and the total weight of jockey, tack and aluminum racing plates. These times adhere to the previously discussed plate weight trend.

With a -0.74 s compensation, each of First Flight's times for the seven LTA distances is slightly below Ruffian's corresponding times, as the table shows.

First Flight's LINEST data which produced these times show her winning 156 total LA points versus 51 points for Landaluce and 57 points for Ruffian.

When First Flight is given a -0.54-s compensation, the situation dramatically changes. Ruffian now wins four of the seven distances, ties one and loses two, as the table shows.

This translates to First Flight winning a total of 93 LA points with Landaluce and Ruffian winning totals of 62 and 127, respectively.

Thus, with just a -0.20 s change in adjusted time, a reversal occurs in the overall winning LA points for Ruffian. Landaluce's total wins are not as drastically affected, changing from 51 to 62.

With a compensation for aluminum racing plates alone given First Flight (no track compensation), the last row of Table 13 shows that Ruffian's times for the seven LA distances are all less than First Flight's.

When 100 randomly simulated match races between only Ruffian and First Flight (because Landaluce's data are barely affected) are run for comparison using this final condition, Ruffian is predicted to win 66/100, 65/100 and 65/100 at 6 f, 8 f and 8.5 f, respectively.

The above considerations show that an extremely fine line exists regarding the propriety of adjusting First Flight's data or not, since there is no obvious scientific way to determine the absolute magnitude of an unbiased adjustment.

The conclusion, certainly open to reader opinion, is to judge that a -0.54 s adjustment to First Flight's data is more than fair. This is at least partially supported by the fact that the time adjustments for aluminum plates, had First Flight worn them, were at the maximum level predicted from the physics formula for kinetic energy, as presented earlier.

At that maximum level, -0.74 s represents roughly an extra -0.45 s allowance, in addition to the aluminum plate adjustment, for slower track conditions which First Flight may have encountered. That condition now needs further investigation.

Belmont Park: Track Conditions in 1946

Since it was shown early in the book that correlations vary widely for different horses regarding how any single factor affects their performance, we do not know whether the Belmont track was *actually slower* when First Flight raced in the mid-1940s than it was during the mid-seventies when Ruffian raced. Many assume it was. We can get a better idea from the following information.

143

The data for at least one comparison are, fortunately, available. The Futurity, a G-2 Stakes Race, has been run at Belmont since 1888. It is for 2YOs. Its distance has varied, but it was run at 6.5 f from 1934 through 1975. This range includes just those years needed to equably compare times for First Flight versus Ruffian.

Surprisingly, the average running time for the Futurity was *shorter* for the decade of the 1940s than it was for the first 6 years of the 1970s decade when it was run at the same distance, 6.5 f. The former average was 75.94 s; the latter average was 76.83 s.

These averages are based on 10 and 6 data values, respectively. The reason for these results is unknown. Nearly everyone would expect and argue that the track conditions of the 1940s were slower.

A t test between the two sets of decade running times shows that they differ significantly, with $\alpha = 0.017$. However, this only substantiates the contention that the running times for the decade of the 1940s were *significantly faster* than those of the 1970s, and not vice versa as might have been expected.

The implied conclusion is that First Flight ran on a track that was faster than or at least as fast as that on which Ruffian ran her two 5.5 f races at Belmont as a 2YO. One of these was a Maiden Special Weights race; the second was the Fashion G-3 Stakes.

Given the above facts, it seems reasonable to say that an extra -0.45 second allowance for track conditions – beyond the allowance for aluminum plates for First Flight – is probably unmerited and that Ruffian was faster than First Flight.

This implies that Landaluce actually was Ruffian's most serious competition as candidate for best 2YO.

Special Comparison: Ruffian and Landaluce

When Ruffian's and Landaluce's LTAs are compared, they show that Landaluce wins the shorter races from 5 f through 6 f and that Ruffian wins the races from 7 f through 8.5 f.

The R^2 values are very high for each filly's LTA. The value is 0.9974 for Ruffian and 0.9998 for Landaluce.

There is, therefore, no reason to suspect that time predictions from the respective LTAs have *much* error associated with them, although some error always exists. The STEYX value, in fact, gives the amount of standard error. It is 0.1885 s for Ruffian and 0.2601 s for Landaluce.

For general comparison purposes, both fillies were extremely well matched regarding race parameters. They each raced five times as 2YOs. Landaluce's races ranged up to 8.5 f, while Ruffian's were from 5.5 f to 6 f.

All their races were on tracks rated fast at the time. Landaluce carried an average of 118.6 lb to Ruffian's 118.0 lb. As we have previously shown, this factor's affect varies greatly from horse to horse and really has no consistent predictability about it. The 0.6 lb difference in this case probably had no effect.

Therefore, it can't be honestly stated that Landaluce was under a slightly greater weight handicap due to the varying effect of this factor amongst Thoroughbreds.

The only point that can be mentioned regarding advantage is that Santa Anita, where Landaluce ran her final two juvenile races, was a generally faster track in the 1980s than were at least some tracks east of the Mississippi.

For instance, the Santa Anita Derby at 9 f was run an average 1.75 s faster throughout the 1980s than were the Blue Grass Stakes at Keeneland or the Wood Memorial at Aqueduct. (7)

However, even if 1.75 s were added to Landaluce's times for the two Santa Anita races, her LTA would still show her as faster than Ruffian at the shorter distances of 5 f, 5.5 f and 6 f.

Adding as much as 1.75 s to Landaluce's times would be unfair because none of her races were as long as 9 f.

Thus, there is no reasonable conclusion other than that Landaluce was probably Ruffian's equal based on the available data. This is one of those instances where the small sample sizes make one uncomfortable in drawing conclusions for fear of showing bias one way or the other.

First Flight, Landaluce and Ruffian, would therefore retain their respective LTA points given in Table 12. The only possible change would be in the LA points.

However, LA points will not be changed, and the current totals will stand. This seems eminently fair, although its deleterious effect on Ruffian's standing should be remembered.

Based on the above considerations, these three fillies are the top candidates for greatest 2YO Thoroughbred of the twentieth century, in the order given in Table 12. Seattle Slew and Affirmed hold the number four and five positions.

The major fault of the BHI rating, based on the point totals just discussed, is that neither First Flight nor Landaluce were apparently even considered as a top-100 horse of the past century, and Ruffian was rated 35th.

Nothing more need be stated regarding the BHI rankings. Finger pointing gains nothing, and the old "hindsight" cliché is poised to rear its ugly head. The BHI ranking was probably not based on a thorough statistical evaluation of the available data.

Selecting the Top 3YOs

Secretariat ranked highest as candidate for best 3YO Thoroughbred of the late nineteenth and early twentieth centuries. There is scant ambiguity in the data.

Table 12 clearly shows the point differences for the top candidate 3YOs based on both LTA and LA scores.

If the total points for 2YO and 3YO Thoroughbreds were combined, Secretariat would be the top candidate for greatest overall Thoroughbred of the past century for these age brackets.Ruffian would rank second, Seattle Slew would rank third and Alydar would rank fourth.

Their respective combined point totals would be: 396, 388, 305 and 303. These values are stated for reference and are not directly given in Table 12.

There are limited ways to interpret small-sample data fairly. Each horse had an equal chance to perform in the brief span of two years, and

Ruffian's performance, as a 2YO is certainly in the top three, if not the best.

Secretariat's total points were clearly the highest among the 3YOs. Probably few people knowledgeable about Thoroughbred racing will truly argue against ranking Secretariat as top candidate for greatest 3YO, although dissenters can always be found.

His Triple Crown races alone show that, when in top form, he was virtually invincible.

His Kentucky Derby time of 119.40 s still represents the standard for that race, with only Monarchos in 2001 coming remotely close to Big Red's time.

Due to a faulty timer and reticence on the part of the Maryland Racing Commission to accept convincing evidence that he had established a new record, Secretariat was denied the Daily Racing Form time for the Preakness, that being 113.40 s.

Such facts aside, there shall always reverberate the undying echoes of those thundering hooves from Elmont, New York on that historic June Saturday in 1973.

Secretariat's Belmont

$$\hat{y} = 97.92x - 3.17$$

For those who demand more subtle proof of his greatness, there forever stands the Belmont, symbolized by that stark and singular equation speaking of greatness with muted eloquence one thousand words must fail to utter.

For those whose souls respond to mathematics as the souls of most mortals harken to music or art, this solitary line, a mathematical Haiku in thirteen ciphers, is both ballade and portrait of the greatest twelve furlongs ever run.

As most Thoroughbred fans know, Secretariat ran the 12-f Belmont in a world-record time, on dirt, of 144.00 s. He did it while looking nonchalant. He averaged twelve seconds per furlong. His record still stands nearly 35 years later.

The allusion to subtlety regarding the Belmont is this: if one takes Secretariat's fractional times for that effort (4 f in 46.20 s, 6 f in 69.80 s, 10 f in 119.00 s and 12 f in 144.00 s) and uses Linear Trend Analysis to generate a mathematically straight line for *that single race*, one can use the result – the singular equation displayed above – to find that Secretariat's time at the 9.5-f point (the Preakness distance) was 113.11 s.

The error in accepting this value will be vanishingly small because the COD of the equation is 0.9999.

Realize that 113.11 s is 0.29 s faster than the **accepted** Preakness record, now shared by Tank's Prospect, Louis Quatorze and Curlin.

In addition, Secretariat broke his own Kentucky Derby record time at the 10-f point of the Belmont by running that distance in 119.00 s.

For that matter, one can substitute 1.625 mi (13 f) for "x", do the indicated math, and find that Secretariat, had he kept his Belmont pace for another furlong, would have broken the current world record on dirt for 13 f (158.20 s by Swaps in 1956 at Hollywood Park) by 2.25 s.

Secretariat actually did unofficially break that world record, according to one observer, by simply continuing a furlong past the finish line on his existing momentum with Ron Turcotte standing in the stirrups!

Thus, further arguments concerning how fast Secretariat actually ran or was capable of running are really academic and superfluous. Perhaps these facts are axiomatically sacrosanct? However, enough has been said and proven. Let us not gild the lily.

It appears that the group of top 3YOs emerging from this study is more realistic than the BHI listing. At least, it is hoped that the major issues in selecting candidate greatest horses have been more clearly presented and definitively stated than formerly.

If there are any real surprises, one might be that Alydar outranked Affirmed (although their point difference is negligible, given the small samples) as a 3YO and that Man o' War scored significantly lower than in the final BHI ranking, even though his times were adjusted in terms of plate weight and presumed slower tracks after the effects of crop sizes were considered.

Although Affirmed beat Alydar (barely) in seven of their nine career matches (he was disqualified in one), Alydar's LTA was actually better than Affirmed's. They were truly close, both in reality and mathematically.

Regarding Man o' War's data, the times for both his 2YO and 3YO races were each liberally adjusted downward to compensate for the combination of presumed slower tracks and the heavier steel plates he wore – both parts of the so-called era differences.

What the rather ambiguous era differences really boil down to, as disclosed by this study, is perhaps a slight track condition influence but a certainly significant performance difference related to the genetics affected by foal crop size.

CB

This concludes the summary of 2YO and 3YO performance data and rankings. The following chapter presents a series of computer-generated match races that should hold great interest for the avid Thoroughbred racing fan.

CHAPTER 13

The notion of time fades gracefully away . . .
-- Christopher Isham

Six Simulated Match Races

It is time to temporarily leave the narrower subject of individual equine greatness and present the results of six special match races that were simulated based upon the best available DRFC data. These should hold great interest for most readers.

Five of these races actually occurred in real life. One, Ruffian's against Foolish Pleasure, ended prematurely and tragically as most fans know. The final match, Secretariat versus Man o' War, is partly speculative based on their data, but it provides food for further intelligent debate at the very least.

The match races are presented chronologically, in the order of their historical occurrence.

Comparison Methods

The final result of each match is based on an average of three analytical techniques used to give a fair and reasonable comparison between each pair of horses.

All races were simulated for 1.25 mi, or 10 f. The average predicted time for 1.25 mi for these simulations was taken from the trend line data of each horse using only data from races held on tracks rated fast *at the time.*

The intent was to display the horse's likely times for various distances to full advantage and thus to estimate the *best likely time* each horse would run 10 f.

The SD for each horse was taken from the Standard Error of Estimate (STEYX) calculated by Excel's LINEST routine. Since all the linear trends had high R^2 values, the randomly generated times based on the LTAs should be truly representative of how the horses likely would have run actual contests.

Method 1: Single Criterion Comparison

Each horse of a given matched pair (e.g., Man o' War and Sir Barton) ran against a *criterion normal distribution, CND*. The average of the CND was the average of the times for the two horses in question at 10 f, and its standard deviation was the average of their STEYX values taken from their LTAs.

Man o' War and Sir Barton were thus matched against their averages, both for overall time and for standard deviation, as were the other pairs of horses.

One-hundred random, computer-generated matches were run for each horse and compared against the described criterion distribution.

Method 2: Individual Distribution Comparisons

One-hundred random matches were computer generated using the actual distribution of *each horse* against that of the second horse, with no averaging criterion involved. This method yields slightly different but important data comparisons.

Method 3: Static Distribution Comparison

Last, a direct single comparison of each horse's distribution for times at 10 f was made. Charts 18 through 23 display these comparisons for each match. Excel's NORMDIST function was used for all static comparisons.

The percent of estimated wins out of 100 hypothetical match races was taken directly from the value derived using the NORMDIST function on these static distributions.

Table 14 shows the number of matches won under each of the three comparisons, by each horse, and the average number of wins estimated by combining the three comparisons.

This three-level approach gives fair and exhaustive comparisons around which future arguments regarding greatness may be centered.

For all cases in Table 14, the horse whose name is highlighted in the first column is the one to whom the win percentages are referenced in each remaining column.

An historical overview of the match race results follows Table 14.

Table 14
Comparisons among Three Simulation Methods: Match Races

Horses	Method 1	Method 2	Method 3	Average
Man o' War – Sir Barton: t = 0.369*	58	56	56	57
Seabiscuit – War Admiral: t = 0.008	59	72	70	67
Swaps – Nashua: t = 0.018	59	69	65	64
Alydar – Affirmed: t = 0.013	43	61	60	55
Ruffian – Foolish Pleasure: t = 0.053	68	82	73	74
Secretariat – Man o' War: t = 0.207	54	60	58	57

*Ten random samples from the 100 distributions, using Method 2, generated for each horse in a matched pair gave the t values shown when their averages were compared. Only values below 0.05 are considered significant. Higher values indicate the horses were essentially equivalent - more correctly stated: that one cannot reject the null hypothesis that the samples representing the two horses came from the same parent population. A borderline value, such as t = 0.053 for Ruffian vs. Foolish Pleasure, is probably significant given the vagaries of small statistical samples.

Match 1: Man o' War vs Sir Barton – 1920

Man o' War was matched against Sir Barton at Kenilworth Race Track in Windsor, Ontario. The date was Tuesday October 12, 1920.

Man o' War was then a 3YO, whereas Sir Barton was a 4YO. There is much speculation that Sir Barton was not totally sound for the race, although details are rather ambiguous other than sore hooves generally being stated.

The track was rated fast and the distance was 1.25 mi. Man o' War, carrying 120 lb, was ridden by Clarence Kummer. Sir Barton's jockey was Frank Keogh, and he carried 126 lb, presumably a justifiable added impost over Man o' War because he was a 4YO.

Man o' War won the race by seven lengths in 123.00 s. It was, thus, not a remotely close contest.

However, using the KE formula to determine how Sir Barton might have fared carrying only 120 lb, as did Man o' War, his time calculates to 121.07 s. Under those circumstances, he would have won by 1.93 s. This projected result is thought provoking, at the very least!

Chart 18 shows the relative placement of the normal distributions representing each horse along the time axis. The results for the Method 3 comparison refer to Chart 18.

Chart 18
Match Race: Man o' War versus Sir Barton

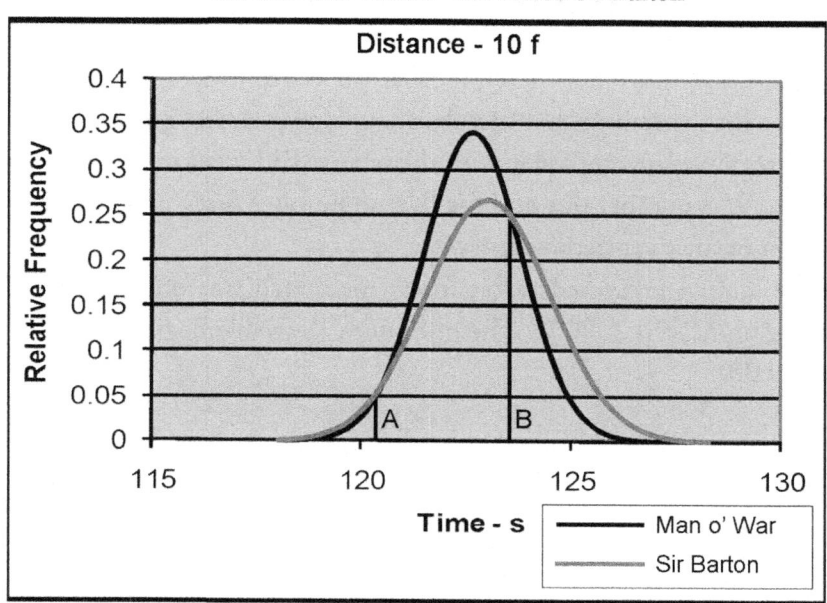

Line A represents 120.50 sec; Line B represents 123.50 sec
Wins in the three graph areas are, within rounding error:
Below A: Man o' War 2; Sir Barton 3
Between A & B: each 29
Above B: Man o' War 25; Sir Barton 12
Total Wins: Man o' War 56; Sir Barton 44
Average simulation wins: Man o' War 57/100

Results

Table 14 shows that the overall average number of wins at 10 f expected by Man o' War over Sir Barton, based on their times for fast tracks at the same respective ages, 3YO, was fifty-seven.

This is actually within the predictability limits of tossing a coin 100 times. Therefore, one cannot say that Man o' War was obviously better. The t score, 0.369 also confirms this judgment. It indicates non-significance between the results of the matches.

No adjustments were necessary for so-called era differences because the two were just a year apart in age.

Man o' War happened to win fairly handily the day they raced, but his trend analysis record by no means overshadows that of Sir Barton's.

Direct comparison of their LTAs suggests that, on average at 10f, Man o' War would win by 1.13 lengths if one could replay numerous races between the two.

All indications are, therefore, that Sir Barton was not performing close to his maximum that October day. However, the general result is not egregiously incompatible with the relative BHI ranking which places Man o' War number one and Sir Barton number forty-nine on the top 100 list of the twentieth century.

An actual preserved ticket from this match was offered on eBay, closing on March 2, 2008. The minimum allowable beginning bid was $1,999.00.

Match 2: Seabiscuit vs War Admiral – 1938

On Tuesday November 1, 1938 these two champions met at Pimlico Race Track (Old Hilltop) in Baltimore, Maryland and raced 1.1875 miles, or 9.5 f.

It is interesting that Seabiscuit was a grandson of Man o' War, and War Admiral was a son of the same champion.

Seabiscuit was a 5YO and War Admiral was a 4YO when they met. Seabiscuit won by four lengths in a time of 116.60 s for the distance on a track rated fast that day.

He carried 120 lbs, as did War Admiral. George (The Iceman) Woolfe was Seabiscuit's jockey and Charlie Kurtsinger was War Admiral's.

Results

The three simulation methods have Seabiscuit winning an average of sixty-seven of 100 matches over 10 f rather than the 9.5 f of their actual match. More complete data are available at 10 f for War Admiral; that is why 10 f was chosen for simulation and LTA rather than the actual 9.5 f.

Chart 19 shows the general relative placement of their individual normal time distributions. The results of the Method 3 comparison refer specifically to Chart 19.

Chart 19
Match Race between Seabiscuit and War Admiral

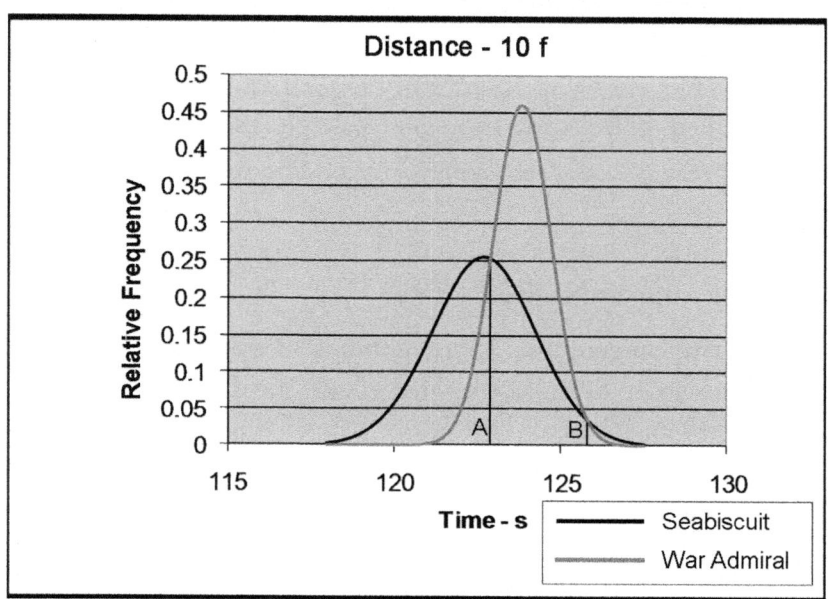

Line A represents 122.75 sec; Line B represents 125.75 sec
Wins in the three graph areas; within rounding error, are:
Below A: Seabiscuit 46; War Admiral 5
Between A & B: 23 each
Above B: Seabiscuit 1; War Admiral 2
Total wins: Seabiscuit 70; War Admiral 30
Average simulation wins: Seabiscuit 67/100

A direct comparison of their time averages for 10 f from LTA gives Seabiscuit an average winning margin of 1.3 lengths.

The results of these matches, both real and simulated, are opposite what the BHI rankings suggest. These results could indicate that War Admiral was not running at his best for the match.

The BHI ranked War Admiral thirteenth and Seabiscuit twenty-fifth among the top 100 Thoroughbreds of the twentieth century. This is, of course, a subjective judgment.

It must *always* be realized that a single match race, unless the results are stunningly apparent, does not prove that one horse is greater than another.

Even children playing games like ping pong or *"round-the-world"* in basketball generally suggest formats such as two-of-three to determine the winner.

Venues like the World Series of baseball and the playoffs of the NBA also realize the same principle working – it is unreasonable to predicate greatness or even superiority on the results of an isolated effort.

Match 3: Swaps vs Nashua – 1955

These two outstanding Thoroughbreds met at Washington Park in Illinois to go 10 f on a track rated good. The date was Wednesday August 31, 1955.

Earlier that year, Swaps beat Nashua in the Kentucky Derby by 1.5 lengths on a fast track in 121.80 s. Swaps did not run in either the Preakness or the Belmont, thus allowing Nashua to win both those remaining Triple Crown races.

Their actual match race result differed from that of the Derby. Nashua won handily at Washington Park by 6.5 lengths in a time of 124.20 s.

Both horses could claim virtually the cream of the crop in their respective jockeys. Willie Shoemaker was aboard Swaps, and Eddie Arcaro rode Nashua. Each carried 126 lb.

Results

The three comparison techniques all agree with the Kentucky Derby results, rather than the match race result.

That is, Swaps averages sixty-four percent of wins over 300 hypothetical, computer-generated matches.

Chart 20 gives a direct comparison of the static normal time distributions of the two horses. The results of the Method 3 comparison pertain directly to Chart 20.

Chart 20
Match Race: Swaps versus Nashua

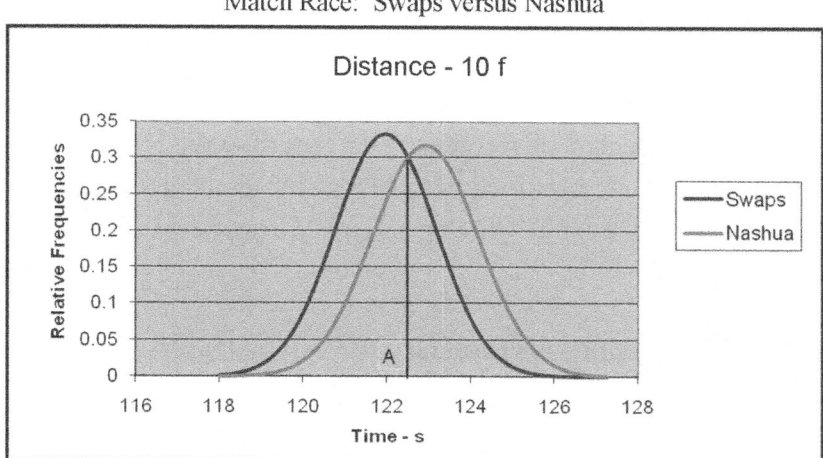

Line A represents 122.5 sec
Wins in the two graph areas are, within rounding error:
Below A: Swaps 49; Nashua 19
Above A: Swaps 16; Nashua 16
Total wins: Swaps 65; Nashua 35
Average simulation wins: Swaps 64/100

The LTA comparison for 10 f, again based only on data each horse established over fast tracks, indicates that Swaps would beat Nashua at that distance by an average of 1.51 lengths.

The BHI rated Swaps twentieth and Nashua twenty-fourth in the top 100 listing. One could say the results of this study basically agree with the qualitative results of the BHI ranking.

Match 4: Affirmed vs Alydar – No specific date

There was no single match race in real life between these horses -- because none was needed!

From 1977 through the 1978 racing seasons, Affirmed faced Alydar, or vice versa as you will, nine times. Affirmed won seven of these races, although barely in many cases.

Affirmed was also disqualified in one race, that of August 19, 1978 at Saratoga. He therefore is officially credited with six wins over Alydar.

Affirmed essentially won the Triple Crown *from Alydar* and no other rival. The horses finishing third behind Alydar in each of the Triple Crown efforts did so by margins of 1.25, 7.5 and 13 lengths in the Kentucky Derby, Preakness and Belmont, respectively.

Alydar thus *placed* an average of 7.25 lengths ahead of his nearest *show* rivals. In fact, Affirmed beat Alydar by an average of just five-eights (0.625) of a length for the Triple-Crown races (about five feet).

An Aside Regarding Secretariat

A comparison is now in order regarding Secretariat, who finished first in this study as the best candidate 3YO of the twentieth century.

Such comparison is not needed to justify the present results, but it certainly lends them substance.

For instance, the comment lines for Affirmed and Alydar in their Triple Crown efforts read: *Fully Extended, Brisk Handling,* and *Driving.* In other words, these horses were going near full throttle, as would be expected for such rivalries and the stakes involved.

In contrast, Secretariat's comment lines for the same three races show: *Handily, Handily,* and *Ridden Out,* each certainly indicating less than maximum effort.

Secretariat also set records in all three races, even though the Maryland Racing Commission *has not* officially acknowledged his Preakness time, contrary to what some Internet web sites proclaim.(16) This point was discussed in the previous chapter.

His times for the trio of races were: 119.40 s, Kentucky Derby; 113.40 s (Daily Racing Form time), Preakness, and 144.00 s, Belmont.

His Derby record has been unequalled in thirty-four years. Monarchos is the only horse to come close. He ran the 2001 Derby in 119.88 s. Secretariat's Belmont time of 144.00 s for the 1.5 mi still stands as the world record for that distance on dirt.

Only Tank's Prospect in 1985, Louis Quatorze in 1996 and Curlin in 2001 have equaled Secretariat's Daily Racing Form Preakness time, but that has been shown earlier to be academic only.

Secretariat's Triple Crown times are thus below Affirmed's for the same races by 1.80 s, 1.00 s and 2.80 s, respectively.

And yes, the tracks were all rated fast for the days on which Affirmed and Alydar ran, as they were for Secretariat. Thus, track arguments are basically irrelevant.

The thoughtful reader may choose to reflect on the implications of the above.

Returning now to Affirmed and Alydar, it is interesting that, if the margins by which either horse won over the other are averaged for their nine mutual meetings, Alydar's average win is actually 1.48 lengths *better* than Affirmed's, even though Affirmed won six of nine races.

This is because Alydar's two winning efforts were by greater margins, 1.25 and 3.5 lengths, than were all but one of Affirmed's.

In four of their races, Affirmed won by margins of nose, head, neck and neck.

Results for Affirmed vs Alydar

In keeping with the closeness of their real-life efforts, the three simulation comparisons show a virtual 50-50 draw based on 300 total random matches.

Chart 21 presents the relative time distributions of Affirmed and Alydar upon which the static comparisons of Method 3 were based.

Chart 21
Match Race: Alydar versus Affirmed

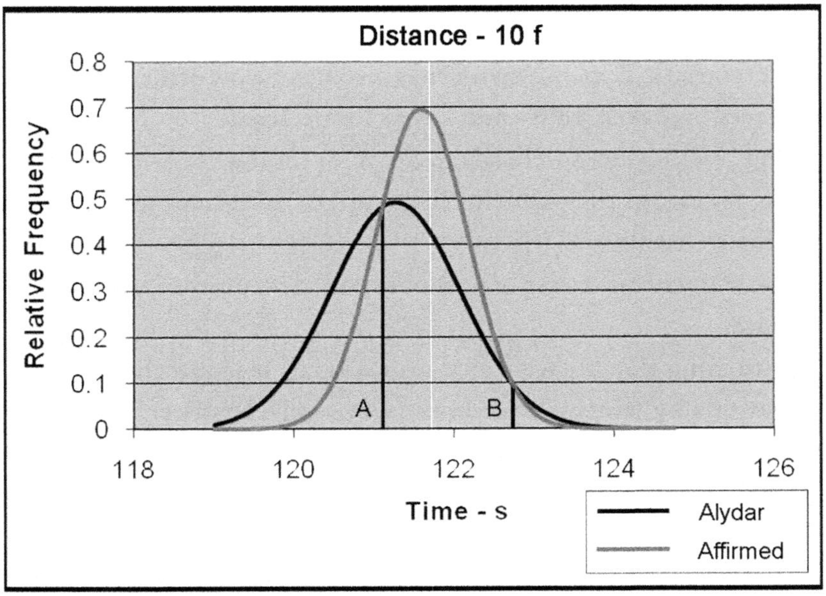

Line A represents 121.25 sec; Line B represents 122.75 sec
Wins in the three graph areas, within rounding error, are:
Below A: Affirmed 13; Alydar 35
Between A & B: 24 wins each
Above B: Affirmed 2, Alydar 1
Total wins: Alydar 60; Affirmed 39; 1 undecided
Average simulation wins: Alydar 55/100

Their LTAs for 10 f also predict that Alydar would win, on average, by 0.49s if they met multiple times at that distance.

As previously stated, Alydar's actual average winning margin, documented in the DRFC past performance lines, was 1.48 lengths for two of nine real-life races.

With numbers this close, it is difficult to say that statistics does not yield valid predictions when it is properly applied.

The t test results run on a sample of size 10 from the Method 2 comparison shows a significant difference at nearly the 0.01 level. This particular comparison also shows Alydar winning the greatest number of matches, sixty-one of 100.

Match 5: Ruffian vs Foolish Pleasure – 1975

On a day that would turn bleak for true Thoroughbred fans, the undisputedly great filly, Ruffian, faced the recent Kentucky Derby winner, Foolish Pleasure.

The setting was Belmont Park. The date was Sunday July 6, 1975. The distance was 10 f, and the track was rated fast.

Jacinto Vasquez, Ruffian's regular jockey, was up, and Braulio Baeza was aboard Foolish Pleasure. The colt carried 126 lb, the filly 121 lb.

Ruffian was undefeated at the time, having won five races the previous year as a 2YO and having won five times during the current year by an average 7.4 lengths.

She was just coming off winning the *filly Triple Crown*, consisting of the Acorn, Mother Goose and CCA Oaks G-1 stakes races when she met Foolish Pleasure.

Foolish Pleasure had won four previous times that year, had placed twice and showed once.

One of his wins was the Kentucky Derby. He was second in the Preakness to Master Derby by 1 length, and he also placed behind Avatar by a neck in the Belmont.

He thus had strong credentials.

As is sadly known, Ruffian broke down before the half-mile call point. She was then leading.

Foolish Pleasure is listed as having finished the race, galloping, in the meaningless time of 122.80 s.

What would have happened had the race been normally completed?

Simulation Results

Quite simply, the three simulation methods predict Ruffian winning seventy-four percent of average, hypothetical efforts against Foolish Pleasure at 10 f.

Chart 22
Match Race: Ruffian versus Foolish Pleasure

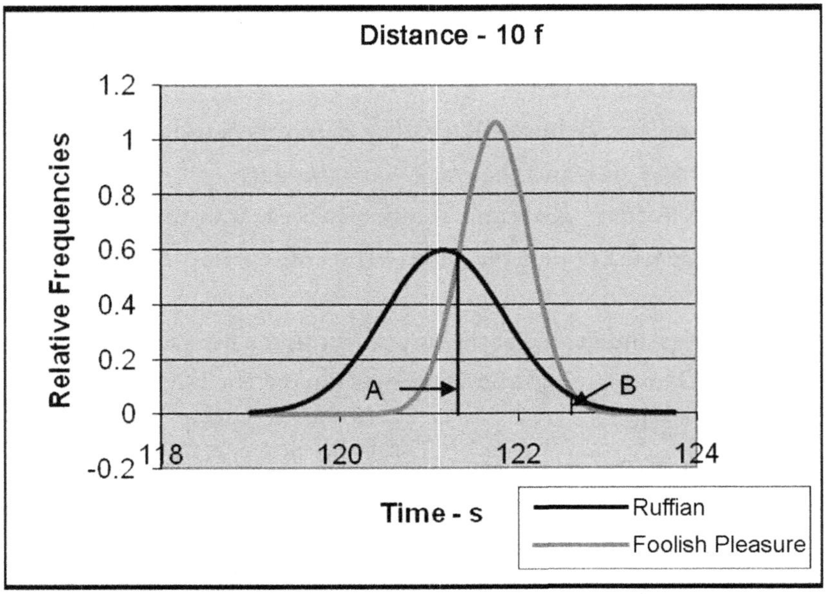

Distance - 10 f

Line A represents 121.25 sec; Line B not applicable due to small area
Wins in the two graph areas, within rounding error, are:
Below A: Ruffian 51; Foolish Pleasure 5
Above A: 22 each
Total wins: Ruffian 73; Foolish Pleasure 27
Average simulation wins: Ruffian 74/100

Chart 22 gives the comparison of normally distributed times for the two horses. The "static" comparison of Method 3 is based on the 100 comparisons implied by this chart.

The LTAs for 10 f predict that Ruffian would likely have won the match, given an average effort from both horses, by 5.6 lengths.

Ruffian is fittingly interred at Belmont Park with her head facing the finish line. It is also fitting, although many would see it only as a result of alphabetical chance, that Ruffian's career record rests on the page opposite and facing, Secretariat's in the DRF Champions 2000 edition.

I prefer to think the Fates assured it being there.

Match 6: Man o' War vs Secretariat – timeless

Man o' War and Secretariat, naturally, never met. Fifty-three years separate the first "Big Red" from the second.

Many fans of each are more than willing to speculate on what would have happened had they raced each other.

From the data available, giving what are considered equitable adjustments for steel racing plates and track conditions of earlier eras to Man o' War, the outcomes are as follows.

Simulation Results

At 10 f on fast tracks, Secretariat is predicted to win fifty-four of 100 races against the criterion normal distribution, Method 1. This result compares to that of tossing a coin. As a reminder, the criterion distribution was characterized by the average of the means and standard deviations of both horses for that distance.

In 100 additional random matches based on their individual distributions of times for 10 f used in the Method 2 comparison, Secretariat was predicted to win an average of sixty matches.

Without time compensation, Man o' War loses eighty-seven of 100 10-f simulations to Secretariat.

Finally, based on a static, single comparison of their respective averages and standard deviations from their LTAs using Method 3, Secretariat was predicted to win fifty-eight of 100 matches.

Chart 23 directly compares the normally distributed time distributions upon which this last estimate was based.

CHART 23
Match Race: Man o' War and Secretariat

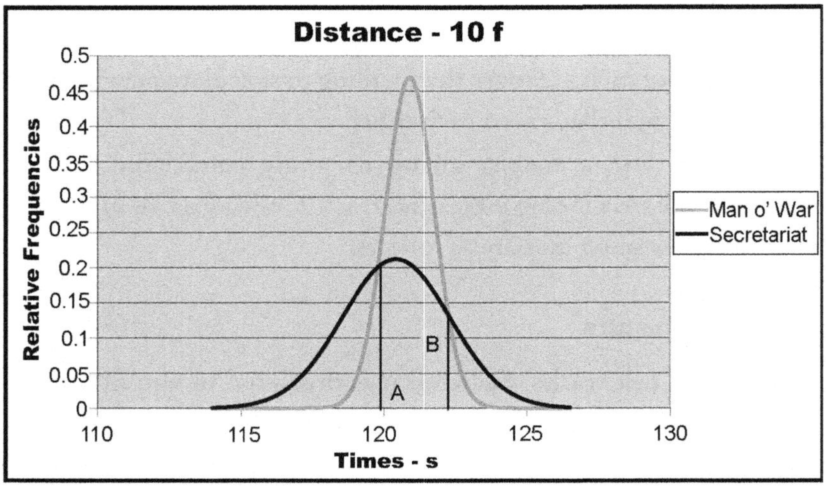

Line A represents 119.80 sec; Line B represents 122.30 sec
Wins in the three graph areas, within rounding error, are:
Below A: Secretariat 32; Man o' War 5
Between A & B: each win 24
Above B: Man o' War 13; Secretariat 2
Total: Secretariat wins 58; Man o' War wins 42
Average simulation wins: Secretariat 57/100

As mentioned several times previous, Man o' War's 3YO times were liberally adjusted to allow for the effects of plate weight and track conditions inimical to speed.

Based on these adjustments, the combined three RNG comparison methods show Secretariat winning an average of fifty-seven of 100 matches. A t test value of 0.207 on ten samples from the Method 2 distributions is not significant. This means that neither horse should be judged better for that distance.

The following facts, however, should indicate that Man o' War cannot be said to have suffered greatly from slower tracks, as opposed to horses of the decade of the 1970s, the era when Secretariat raced.

For example, as documented previously, Ours (23), states that Belmont's surface was upgraded in August 1918, as was Saratoga's by May of 1919.

Therefore, both tracks were faster than tracks typical of the era when Man o' War raced on them – in 1919 and 1920.

It was also shown previously that foal crop contributes at least a factor of 0.83 to the decline in average running times over the decades of the twentieth century, based on data from the Kentucky Derby, the Preakness, the Belmont, the Santa Anita Derby and the general foal crop trend.

In fact, the difference in the Belmont's average running time for the final four years of the 1920s (when the Belmont was run at 1.5 mi) and the entire decade of the 1970s was 3.87 s. Multiplying 0.83 by 3.87 gives 3.21 s.

If 3.21 s (foal crop effect) is subtracted from each of the earlier Belmont running times and a t test is done between the resulting times for the last four years of the 1920s and the ten years of the 1970s, no significant difference exists. That is, the generally presumed surface inequality vanishes.

The level-of-significance value, α, for that case is 0.224. One generally requires an α level of 0.05 *or less* to indicate a significant difference between two samples.

Therefore, foal crop changes alone can account for the stated decade time differences, and no need to invoke track conditions arises.

Second, an easy way to compare the two horses, *free from any era effect – imagined or otherwise –* is simply to calculate what is termed the *z score* for each horse.

The z score compares only the relative performance of each horse against *his peers*, not against the horses of another era. Therefore, no bias exists because all the era components that might have existed are automatically factored out.

When this is done, Man o' War's Belmont z score for the decade of the 1920s is -1.71. This indicates that his time for the Belmont was about 1.7 standard deviations better than the average for his peers.

Secretariat's Belmont z score for the 1970s was -1.87. This places him slightly better in relation to his peers than was Man o' War to his.

Also remember that Secretariat undoubtedly faced greater competition in his era. The competition stemmed from foal crop size alone, other factors aside.

I believe, therefore, that the case is sufficiently established that Secretariat was the faster horse when compared to Man o' War, as great as the latter was for his time.

Concluding Remarks

The following chapter uses LTA exclusively to select the best 4YO and 5YO Thoroughbreds from the late nineteenth through the twentieth centuries.

This approach streamlines the analysis by eliminating the data sort and LA. At this level, it takes nothing from the veracity of the results, based on the previous analyses.

The main thrust of this book was to identify the candidate greatest 2YOs and 3YOs. That has been accomplished.

However, many great horses raced beyond their juvenile and sophomore years, some not coming into their own until their fourth or fifth year. This should not be surprising, since horses are not considered fully mature until age five.

It is thus proper to select the candidates for best 4YO and 5YO without prolonged data analyses which might detract from the analyses of the 2YOs and 3YOs.

A good sampling of candidate 4YOs and 5YOs has been chosen. It is unlikely that an outstanding horse has been overlooked by this abbreviated process.

After the LTA results for these older horses are presented, a special chapter on a truly special filly follows.

A summary and epilog chapter then closes this study of Thoroughbred greatness.

CHAPTER 14

Time travels in divers places with divers persons. I'll tell you who Time ambles withal, who Time trots withal, who Time gallops withal, and who he stands still withal.
-- William Shakespeare

Linear Trend Results: Four-Year-Olds

Twenty-two horses, of the top 100 ranked by BHI, Inc., were selected for LTA to determine the candidate greatest performing 4YO. The lowest ranked of these twenty-two was Lady's Secret, number seventy-six.

Gun Bow, selected as a "wild card," was not ranked by the BHI group but had strong credentials. He was among the champion horses listed in the DRFC.

Neither Man o' War nor Secretariat raced beyond their third year.

At this point in the study, it was felt that no further analysis than LTA was needed to fairly separate the horses regarding ability to run standard distances common to the older age groups (4YOs and 5YOs).

The final top ten 4YO horses (plus one tie) are listed in Table 15. The table includes their final ranking and the four principal parameters of their LTAs: slope, intercept, R^2, and STEYX.

Each horse was compared with the others at eleven distances ranging from 0.625 mi (5 f) to 1.625 mi (13 f). These distances were most typical of those run by 4YOs.

The maximum LTA points a given horse could earn was 242. That is, twenty-two points were awarded to first place for each of the distances run. This follows the same point – assignment format as for the 2YOs and 3YOs.

Table 15

Final Linear Trend Results for Four-Year-Olds

Horse	Rank/ Points	Slope	Intercept	COD (R²)	STEYX
Spectacular Bid	1/211	107.18	-13.63	0.9886	1.4591
Dr. Fager	2/203	106.12	-12.19	0.9946	1.2790
Swaps	3/199	102.50	-8.14	0.9942	1.5614
Affirmed	4/195	104.70	-10.44	0.9962	1.2628
Seattle Slew	5/176	103.47	-8.85	0.9982	1.0521
Alysheba	6/169	103.85	-9.16	0.9169	1.8422
Native Dancer	7/160	93.60	2.03	0.9959	1.0614
Forego	7/160	106.09	-11.48	0.9996	0.6783
Lady's Secret	8/150	110.78	-16.51	0.9816	1.1447
Buckpasser	9/145	107.91	-13.13	0.9998	0.3536
Round Table	10/130	101.10	-5.36	0.9743	1.5488

The high average R^2 value (0.9884) for the twenty-two horses indicates an excellent fit of the linear trend lines to the data and renders predictions from the trend lines accurate.

In fact, fourteen of the twenty-two horses had R^2 values above 0.99. It is worthwhile to repeat that these high values imply that the straight line trends fit the data with over 99% accuracy.

The Table 15 results indicate that Spectacular Bid ranks highest as candidate for best 4YO Thoroughbred of the twentieth century.

The eleven horses listed in Table 15 were also rewarded with proportional points for weight carried. However, this did not change the rankings. The highest average weight, 133.25 lb, was carried by Dr. Fager.

As was true for the 2YOs and 3YOs, the time in which a given horse is predicted to run a given distance, within the stated limits for Table 15, is calculated by multiplying that distance in miles by the slope factor in column three and then adding the intercept factor from column four.

Dr. Fager's "Hole-in-the-Wind" Mile

An interesting example is provided by calculating Dr. Fager's predicted time for the mile by multiplying 1.00 mi by 106.12 and then adding -12.19 (adding a negative number is the equivalent of subtracting).

The result is: $1 \cdot (106.12) - 12.19 = 93.93$ s. Dr. Fager's fastest time for the mile was actually 92.20 s set at Arlington Park on Saturday August 24, 1968.

His time is still the world record on dirt, having been tied only once on Wednesday May 7, 2003 by Najran. However, Najran carried just 113 lb – 21 lb less than the Dr!

Dr. Fager's STEYX value, last column of Table 15, is 1.279. It is easily seen that 93.93 s – 92.20 s = 1.73 s. This time is well within $\pm$ 2 STEYX ($\pm$ 2.558) of Dr. Fager's world record time.

Thus, the prediction equation works well even at this extreme limit – a "hole in the wind" as many horsemen refer to exceptional speed – of a world record.

⚃

Interesting results were obtained when 100 randomly generated match races between the final top five 4YOs were simulated.

The 4YO match races followed the same format as the 3YO matches. The means and SDs for 10 f, as obtained from the individual linear trends, were used in Excel's RNG routine to generate the 100 match races.

The horses compared were, in the rank order they finished the LTA, Spectacular Bid, Dr. Fager, Swaps, Affirmed and Seattle Slew.

The winner of each match was determined by finding which of the five horses had the minimum time for each match and adding the number of minimum times the given horse had for all 100 matches. Table 16 presents a partial list of the first thirty-one simulations of 100 with the minimum times highlighted.

Table 16
A Sample of the 100 Match Races between 4YOs
T test results included*

Spectacular Bid	Dr. Fager	Swaps	Affirmed	Seattle Slew	Swaps	Seattle Slew
119.90	121.30	119.89	121.42	121.86	119.89	121.86
118.48	120.03	121.88	120.45	122.93	121.88	122.93
120.70	120.27	117.43	119.79	119.05	117.43	119.05
122.20	119.69	122.45	119.48	120.02	122.45	120.02
122.09	120.26	122.28	119.85	121.15	122.28	121.15
122.87	117.60	117.77	120.59	120.12	117.77	120.12
117.15	120.29	120.08	120.58	120.82	120.08	120.82
120.00	118.76	119.32	119.73	121.52	119.32	121.52
121.94	120.66	119.71	117.72	120.40	119.71	120.40
118.75	121.10	118.20	118.39	120.64	118.20	120.64
119.33	122.14	122.34	120.62	120.37	122.34	120.37
117.87	119.67	121.37	122.07	120.17	121.37	120.17
117.65	119.50	121.37	120.85	121.51	131.37	121.51
118.91	120.65	121.27	120.83	122.61	121.27	122.61
119.21	120.16	120.96	119.69	122.81	120.96	122.81
117.25	120.19	119.02	120.17	120.17	119.02	120.17
119.51	122.48	117.76	118.99	119.82	117.76	119.82
119.75	120.51	120.08	121.59	121.61	120.08	121.61
120.54	120.27	121.07	119.40	120.44	121.07	120.44
119.81	122.80	118.87	119.94	120.67	118.87	120.67
119.86	119.65	116.75	120.18	120.17	116.75	120.17
119.80	122.09	118.64	117.45	120.01	118.64	120.01
122.30	120.44	117.55	120.14	118.51	117.55	118.51
120.22	120.38	122.95	120.35	121.49	122.95	121.49
120.07	122.52	118.47	121.16	120.91	118.47	120.91
119.59	120.92	122.39	120.35	119.29	122.39	119.29
123.22	121.02	120.40	121.66	120.35	120.40	120.35
121.60	120.16	123.56	118.37	118.27	123.56	118.27
123.81	121.33	118.59	120.33	118.67	118.59	118.67
119.38	120.37	120.13	121.01	119.95	120.13	119.95
122.76	119.52	118.62	119.22	120.19	t test:	0.129

*minimum values shaded

Of these 100 simulated match races, the following numbers of wins were obtained: Spectacular Bid 28/100; Swaps 29/100; Dr. Fager 15/100; Affirmed 15/100; Seattle Slew 13/100.

These results are inconclusive. That is, one cannot say that one horse was superior at 10 f to the others from the total number of wins, even though Swaps and Spectacular Bid had nearly twice as many wins as Dr. Fager and Affirmed.

To substantiate this conclusion, a t test was run between thirty-one of the randomly generated times for Swaps and Seattle Slew, the horses having the greatest spread in total wins, twenty-nine versus thirteen.

Even at that level of difference, the value of alpha for the test was 0.129, as Table 16 shows. This value is not significant regarding the difference in the means of either horse for a sample of size thirty-one.

Since a sample size of thirty or more is considered large, the conclusion must be that no significant difference in running 10 f is evident among these five horses, even though Spectacular Bid's LTA showed the fastest overall times at the most distances.

This is a prime example of how one must be cautious in claiming the superiority of one horse over another. It simply cannot be fairly done on the results of a single race, which is all that is usually granted in real life.

This point was made previously in the case of Affirmed and Alydar. The large number of random, unknown factors influencing the outcome of any given race simply negates the possibility of judging one horse superior on that basis alone. The reader is again referred to Excursus E regarding a perspective on factors influencing race outcomes.

Spectacular Bid – A Closer Look

One final but critical point must be mentioned. Of the 100 simulated 4YO matches, the fastest time was generated for Spectacular Bid on the 51st trial. It was 116.58 s, or 1:56:58 in more standard notation.

If this sounds like a ridiculously fast time, consider that Spectacular Bid actually holds the world record for 10 f on dirt. He set it in the

Charles H. Strub Stakes at Santa Anita in 1980. His time then was 1:57:80 s.

Spectacular Bid's standard deviation, as determined from his LTA, is 1.459. Since his LTA mean value for 10 f is 120.34 s, he could theoretically run as fast as 115.96 s for 10 f. That time represents the minus-three-sigma level.

His world record value is actually -1.74 SD below his mean value. The time of 116.58 s generated for this study represents -2.58 SD. Thus, the computer simulations are realistic in terms of possible real-world performances.

Linear Trend Results: Five-Year-Olds

The results of the LTA for 5YOs are shown in Table 17. The same format is used as in Table 16 for the 4YOs.

Table 17
Results of Linear Trend Analysis for Five-Year-Olds

Horse	Rank/Points	Slope	Intercept	COD (R^2)	STEYX
Forego	1/116	106.12	-11.93	0.9991	0.7123
Citation	2/105	101.93	-6.74	0.9976	1.7296
Noor*	3/100	107.10	-12.54	0.9959	2.1007
Skip Away	4/95	111.48	-17.46	0.9707	1.2936
Cigar	5/93	97.10	-0.89	0.9672	1.3465
Round Table	6/84	107.74	-12.65	0.9960	2.0989
Kelso	7/73	104.40	-8.29	0.9982	1.3458
John Henry	8/60	98.38	-0.64	0.9100	5.3306
Seabiscuit	9/54	106.76	-10.22	0.9846	1.7942
Equipoise	10/53	109.41	-13.11	0.9985	1.5741
Discovery	11/35	113.31	-16.49	0.9955	1.3984
Exterminator	12/26	109.07	-11.07	0.9914	4.3937
Phar Lap	13/16	110.00	-11.54	0.9946	2.6701

*No time adjustments, as indicated in text.

The 5YOs were compared via LTA at ten distances typical of those at which they most frequently ran in actual races. The distances ranged from 6 f to 16 f.

Since thirteen 5YOs were selected for the LTA, 130 total points were possible, as opposed to the 242 points for eleven distances at which the 4YOs were compared.

The set of comparisons among the 5YOs yields a problem similar to that between Ruffian and First Flight as 2YOs. That is, Noor raced as a 5YO in 1950. He thus could be credited with a maximum -0.74 s on each of his times, but there is a question whether he then is overcompensated.

Noor, an Irish Thoroughbred, had a remarkable record as a 5YO, even without compensation. He raced twelve times in 1950. His overall win, place and show record was 7-4-1.

In six of his twelve races he ran impressive times which equaled or bettered the existing track record. His SRs for these six races, as given in the DRFC, are: 101, 101, 108, 104, 127 and 106.

He was assigned just 117 lb and 110 lb, respectively, for these latter two races, but his imposts for the other four races ranged from 123 lb to 130 lb.

It should be noted that Noor met Citation in five of his twelve 5YO races and won four. However, he only beat Citation by a nose in the San Juan Capistrano 14 f race. Noor's SR for that race was 127. However, Noor carried only 117 lb to Citation's 130 lb.

A KE calculation shows that, had Citation carried 117 lb, he could theoretically have run the same distance in 8.85 s less! Citation's time conceivably could have been 163.95 s for generating the same amount of KE.

Citation was also known not to have been in peak form during his entire 5YO season and probably should not have raced.

Such remarks aside, the question of how much time to compensate Noor for the fact that he wore steel racing plates and possibly ran on slower tracks in 1950 is important to the outcome of the LTA for 5YOs.

Belmont Park, Roseben and Secretariat

Another crucial observation relating to track conditions is now presented. It may seem roundabout, but it bears on the present question. It involves data of races run in 1906 and 1973. The respective horses in question are Roseben (The Big Train) and Secretariat.

Roseben was an absolutely splendid Thoroughbred who ran 111 career races spanning ages two through eight. He was not ranked among the top 100 in the BHI poll, but probably should have been. He was foaled in 1901 and finally amassed a record of 52-25-12 out of his 111 starts. Very impressive!

The important race, for impact on this study, is Roseben's October 16, 1906 7 f at Belmont. The track was fast, and Roseben covered the distance in a swift 1:22:00 s, or 82.00 s while carrying 126 lb. It took forty-one years for that record to fall.

By generating a single LTA for Secretariat's Belmont of 1973, as was done in Chapter 12, using the major call point distances and times as independent and dependent variables, respectively, one can then accurately compute that Secretariat's 7 f mark was reached in 82.51 s.

This result is probably accurate at the 99.99% level due to the extremely high COD of the resultant linear trend line.

Secretariat was, therefore, about one-half second slower at the 7 f point for the same track than was Roseben some sixty-seven years earlier, amazing as that may sound.

Of course Secretariat would obviously have been running faster if the race was only 7 f, but this brings up the critical point regarding track conditions.

Roseben's performance earned an SR of 116 on a day when the Track Variant (TV) was 00. Thus, by definition of TV, the track was running average for all horses on that day at that distance.

Secretariat's Belmont performance earned an SR of 113 on a day when the TV was 05. Thus, for all races that day, Belmont was running about 1 s below average (the reader is reminded that a TV of 05 implies the track is slower by five-fifths of a second, or 1.0 s).

The point is that, if Belmont was truly running 1.0 s slower than average on that June 9 day in 1973, then Secretariat may well have reached the 7 f point in about 82.00 s, the same time Roseben ran on the same track 67 years previous.

And if all the above argument is internally consistent, then the intrinsic track speed in 1906 may have been nearly identical to what it was in 1973.

Noor: Assessment at age Five

Noor ran three of his twelve 5YO races of 1950 at Belmont, and so the above implication – that he certainly should not be compensated for these three races – is now at least viable.

If Noor is uncompensated for *any* of his races, then Forego beats him at all distances. If Noor is given the maximum compensation of -0.74 s per race, the propriety of which is at least debatable, then Noor wins at distances from 6 f to 10 f and Forego wins at distances from 12 f to 16 f.

A slight downward adjustment, intermediate to the above two extremes, in Noor's time will have Forego winning at more than half the distances.

The inclination, based on Noor's outstanding record, is to say that he was possibly equivalent to Forego as a 5YO (his record as a 4YO was not stellar) but that in this case the data are too sparse and the statistics of small samples are just unstable enough to allow making a strong statistical case one way or the other.

Since the objective here is to attempt an unbiased judgment on the *candidate* greatest horses at given ages, I will rank Forego first, Citation second, and Noor an extremely close third. It could easily be otherwise.

In passing, it is noted that Noor was ranked sixty-ninth by the BHI panel. This probably is too low an assessment of Noor, at least as a 5YO.

Based upon the 5YO LTA analyses, the top five candidate horses (alphabetically) for greatest 5YO Thoroughbred of the twentieth century are: Cigar, Citation, Forego, Noor, and Skip Away.

Note again that it is only feasible to compare horses confidently using LTA because the CODs are as high as they are.

In nine of thirteen cases for 5YOs, the COD was 0.99 or higher, while for 4YOs it was 0.99 or higher in seven of ten cases. Its lowest value, for John Henry as a 5YO, was 0.91. Even this value is extremely high for essentially randomly determined data. Most researchers in other academic areas seldom, if ever, find CODs this high.

Simulated Match Races: Five-Year-Olds

Two sets of 100 simulated match races (200 total) each between the top five 5YO candidates were run. However, the results were ambiguous due to both the closeness of the data among horses and the uncertainty in the proper amount of compensation for Noor.

The simulated wins for each horse were: Forego 37, Citation 57, Noor 37, Skip Away 11 and Cigar 58. However, a t test of 30 mean running times generated from one set of 100 simulations between Cigar and Forego was insignificant. Its value was alpha = 0.421.

Thus, even though Cigar and Citation won twenty more simulated races than Forego, their mean times were not significantly different when compared statistically.

Based on the above discussion, a table of simulation results is not presented for the 5YOs.

A Shapiro-Wilk test of normalcy was run on the actual DRFC times for 10 f by Cigar, Citation, Forego, Noor and Skip Away. The respective p values were: 0.342, 0.443, 0.192, 0.070 and 0.339.

These values indicate that the distributions of run times for 10 f for the five horses were normal. Noor's value might be considered borderline, but technically it meets normalcy. A p value below 0.05 is necessary for non-normalcy.

Noor's value aside, it appears safe to compare the corresponding distributions via RNG simulations and LA, and the above results should be considered acceptable.

Seabiscuit Helps Verify Results

Again, as for the 4YOs, it is instructive to select one horse, in this case Seabiscuit is chosen, and see how the numbers predicted by his trend equation for a given distance compare with reality.

On Tuesday November 1, 1938 Seabiscuit met War Admiral, then a 4YO, for a 9.5 f, match at Pimlico in Baltimore, Maryland. The track was fast and each horse carried 120 lb. Although discussed previously, a few additional and pertinent comments are due this match.

Seabiscuit's 5YO LTA, not shown in Table 15 since he ranked below the top 10, predicts that for 9.5 f his time would be: $1.1875 \cdot (106.76) -10.22 = 116.56$ s. His actual time versus War Admiral was 116.60 s. This prediction represents an error of just 0.034 percent!

It is also well within Seabiscuit's standard error of estimate, STEYX, which is 1.79 s, rounded to two decimal places.

War Admiral's linear trend for age four predicts that he would run the same distance race, 9.5 f, in a time of:

$1.1875 \cdot (105.28) - 7.52 = 117.49$ s.

This means he would have finished in a predicted time difference of $117.49 - 116.56 = 0.93$ s behind Seabiscuit, according to their linear trend analyses.

Their actual finishing time difference, according to the estimation method presented earlier in this book and based on their DRFC race times was 0.60 s, rounded to two decimal places.

This one-third second time difference between prediction and reality is, I submit, extraordinary considering it is based on a small sample gathered sixty-nine years ago!

☙

This concludes the data analyses for the 4YOs and 5YOs. In the following chapter the biography of a very special Thoroughbred is presented. Her record, in fact, makes us reevaluate much of what has preceded herein.

The final chapter then presents an overview/epilog regarding what this book has attempted to accomplish and what has been discovered herein that hopefully will be valuable to Thoroughbred racing enthusiasts, both amateur and professional, in future studies.

CHAPTER 15

We have no reason to think that even now time is quite perfectly continuous and uniform in its flow.
-- C. S. Pierce

A QUINTESSENTIAL THOROUGHBRED

Kincsem's Remarkable Record

On Tuesday March 17, 1874 an event in Kisber, Hungary occurred which could render all that has preceded in this book inconsequential, at best.

That day a female foal, colored liver-chestnut, entered life by the sire Cambuscan, owned by none other than Queen Victoria, out of the dam Water Nymph. She was a direct descendent of the Darley Arabian.

This filly would eventually be named "Kincsem," meaning "my treasure" in Hungarian.

And Kincsem was indeed to become the treasure of her owner and breeder, Ernst von Blaskovich, and of her trainer, Robert Hesp.

She would race fifty-four total times between the ages of two and five. Of these fifty-four efforts she would win them all!

There was simply no question of place, show, or being off the board for Kincsem.

In her juvenile year, 1876, she raced ten times. Six of these efforts were in Germany, two were in Hungary, and one each was in Austria and Czechoslovakia. She ran at distances from 4.5 f to 8 f.

Kincsem's average rest between races that year was 14.44 days. In three of the ten races she distanced the field. Her average winning margin for the remaining seven races was 4.07 lengths, and she carried an average weight, excluding racing plates, of 122.2 lb.

Things improved during her sophomore year, but not for her rivals. She faced seventeen adversaries, both colts and fillies. Again, she won all seventeen races. Now the distances ranged from 8 f to 16 f.

Seven of these races were in Hungary, four were in Austria, four were in Germany, including the prestigious Grosser Preis von Baden, and two were in Czechoslovakia.

Her average rest period between races was just 11.19 days. She carried an average weight of 121.7 lb and won thirteen of these races by an average margin of 4.27 lengths. In two events she distanced the field. She had two walkovers because her reputation was growing and other competitors were staying clear. In three races she won by ten lengths.

The stars were also favorably aligned in the year 1878 for Kincsem. She entered fifteen races at age four and won them all. The distances increased to between 8 f and 20 f.

This, her third racing year, found her in England and France once each. She captured the Goodwood Cup in England and the Grand Prix de Deauville in France by two lengths and one-half length, respectively.

Her remaining thirteen races of 1878 centered around more familiar surroundings: Austria five times, Hungary seven times, and Germany once. Czechoslovakia was skipped that year.

Kincsem enjoyed an average of 13.07 days rest for the 1878 campaign. She won eleven of these races by an average margin of 2.45 lengths. She had her only career close call, by finishing in a dead heat with Prince Giles the First, in the Grosser Preis von Baden.

For that effort she carried 137.5 lb to his 122 lb. As though miffed at her earlier performance, she beat him "decisively," as it is described, in the ensuing run-off.

She distanced the field three times in 1878 and had one walkover.

For the 1878 campaign, Kincsem carried an average of 144.9 lb, obviously an unimaginable burden by modern weight-for-age standards within handicap racing.

The culmination year 1879 saw Kincsem turn five years old and, by definition, reach full maturity. It would be her final racing year. She was now no longer a filly but a mare.

She disappointed none with her performances, winning twelve times in twelve starts by an average margin of 4.6 lengths and carrying an average impost of 153.3 lb. Yes, that is the accurate figure! Her competition distances ranged from 12 f to 18 f.

The lowest weight she ran under as a 5YO was 136 lb while her heaviest impost was 168 lb. Try as they might, the racing stewards simply could not force her to lose.

That final year must have been somewhat disappointing to her breeder-owner and to her trainer because she did not manage to distance the field, even once. Apparently the outlandish imposts accomplished something.

She did, however, enjoy three walkovers. Her average rest period between races for the year was 16.0 days. These generous respites undoubtedly made her feel somewhat like a slacker.

⍦

Times must certainly exist for some of Kincsem's races, but this author has been thus far unable to obtain them, despite having contacted several authorities within various countries where she raced.

The British Racing Authority, for example, indicated they did not have times going back to the 1878 Goodwood Cup.

Several authorities failed to respond to the requests for time information. Such is the state of modern life.

Nonetheless, it is known that times going back to at least 1846 exist for the Epsom Derby, run in 2:55.00 s(8). Therefore, Kincsem must have been timed in at least some races. Unfortunately, she did not race in the Epsom Derby.

Kelso and the Jockey Club Gold Cup

Let us, then, use the information from one well-known American race to estimate the time and the momentum that Kincsem might easily have generated, assuming that she at least equaled the average time for the same distance race and knowing the weight she carried.

Between 1921 and 1975 the American Jockey Club Gold Cup (JCGC) was run at 16 f or 2 miles. This is the same distance Kincsem ran in the Grosser Preis von Baden, and they are both flat races, contrary to many European races.

During that fifty-four-year span, the fastest time for the JCGC was achieved by Kelso in 1964. His time was 3:19.20 s, or 199.20 s.

Kelso carried 124 lb, not including plate weight, for the race. It is easily calculated that Kelso's average speed was 53.01 ft/s.

Kelso's momentum, therefore, was the product of his average speed and the weight he carried, or 6573.5 units.

During those same fifty-four years, the slowest time for the JCGC was 3:27.40 s (207.40 s) by Pot o' Luck in 1945.

The correlation between weight carried and time run for the JCGC for those years, as determined by Excel's CORREL application, was -0.142.

Contrary to expectation and common sense, this represents an *inverse* relationship between weight and time. It means that as weight carried increased, the times decreased. Or, vice versa, as weight decreased, the times increased. Neither condition makes obvious sense.

The result is consistent, however, with the earlier findings regarding Dr. Fager's correlation between weight carried and time run. That number was -0.323.

This highlights the problem mentioned earlier – that presumed correlations people tend to cite are not generally proven by reality. Just because a horse is assigned higher weight does not necessarily mean it will run slower in a given race.

The weight range for this series of fifty-four JCGC races was between 114 lb and 125 lb. Thus, we can conclude that an eleven-lb weight range does not necessarily affect performance significantly. This surely must be related to that old physics principle, paraphrased, "Anything that is not strictly forbidden may happen."

In fact, the squared correlation coefficient $(-0.142)^2$ yields the value 0.020. When multiplied by 100, this number indicates that the given correlation explains only 2% of the relationship between weight carried and running time for the given distance.

Considering the preceding facts, let us argue as follows:

Assume that Kincsem ran the 16-f Grosser Preis von Baden (GPVB) in a slightly slower time than the slowest Jockey Club Gold Cup was run during the subject fifty-four-year time span at two miles.

Assume, therefore, that she ran the GPVB, at age 3, in 3:28.00 s, or 208.00 s.

Kincsem carried 137.5 lb in that race. Therefore, her momentum then calculates to 6980.80 units, since her average speed was 50.77 ft/s. That momentum figure easily exceeds the momenta of all the colts or fillies in the present study – both at 2 mi and 1.5 mi!

The only close figure at 1.5 mi is Secretariat's 1973 Belmont effort in which he generated 6972.9 units of momentum and set the world record for the distance on dirt, which still stands.

To reiterate, Kelso's average speed for his fastest JCGC was 53.01 ft/s, and his momentum was 6573.50 units. This momentum is well below Kincsem's, given the assumed numbers.

Conclusions Regarding Kincsem

Based on the preceding, there may be valid objections concerning Kincsem's ability to generate greater momentum than Kelso at 2 mi or Secretariat at 1.5 mi. Therefore, assume her momentum in the GPVB equaled Kelso's in the JCGC.

Since she carried 11.5 lb more weight than Kelso, using the momentum formula (the KE formula may also be used) $6573.50 = w \cdot v$ gives Kincsem a speed of 47.81 ft/s. Her time for 16 f would then be 220.89 s, or 3:40.89 s.

It is probable that she ran faster than the slowest JCGC time, but the above certainly puts a modestly accurate limit on where her speed and times fell, lacking actual numbers.

All time or speed questions aside, it is obvious from her record that Kincsem was a special Thoroughbred.

Even if half of her matches were below the modern G-3 level, which is difficult to judge, she had to be enormously healthy and fit to endure the travel and competition levels she faced. She had to want to win.

Remember that even Man o' War lost once, and Secretariat lost five times, in their careers.

Granting that excuses can always be offered for those losses, the record books nonetheless coldly display their wares.

Can one claim that every horse that either Man o' War or Secretariat faced was in the same class and truly provided honest competition? Hardly!

Considering the schedule she kept, the distances she ran and the weights she carried, I completely agree with equine authorities such as Richard Sowers that ". . . the enormous imposts she carried – often 25 or 35 more pounds than today's best handicap horses will shoulder in their lives – and the punishing distances at which she competed, often against males, leave little question that the filly whose name means "my treasure" in Hungarian compares favorably with any thoroughbred [sic] in history." (27)

ॐ

Monuments to Greatness

As time, the great final arbiter, would arrange it, Kincsem suffered a colic attack shortly after foaling the Doncaster filly, Kincs.

The great Kincsem thus ironically died on her birth anniversary, Thursday March 17, 1887. She was thirteen.

Among Kincsem's honors are the Kincsem Horse Park in Budapest, Hungary, the Kincsem Museum in Budapest, the Kincsem Farm in Archer, Florida, a life-sized statue of her at Kincsem Park, Budapest and, perhaps most significantly, a statue at the entrance to Keeneland Race Course in Lexington, Kentucky.

No true Kentuckian can be said not to value or recognize a truly great horse.

And, fortunately, unlike the case for prophets, Kincsem was amply honored in both her home and other countries.

CHAPTER 16

Gather ye rosebuds while ye may; Old Time is still a-flying.
-- Robert Herrick

Summary and Purpose of the Study

The main purpose of this book was to select the candidate greatest horse, or horses, of the late nineteenth through the twentieth centuries using basic statistics.

The techniques for accomplishing the task included a data sort, Linear Trend Analysis and Limits Analysis. Each of the three techniques was applied at age levels two and three. Linear Trend Analysis and Limits Analysis were applied at ages four and five.

It is realized that imperfections exist in any statistical study. Tradeoffs nearly always are necessary, and not everyone reading the results will agree with them.

The only alternatives, however, are gut-level feelings or other visceral types of judgment. These simply will not do. Such feelings have not achieved a rapprochement regarding Thoroughbred greatness after decades, and they will not succeed in present times when everybody seems to hail from Missouri.

The techniques applied herein are no exception to that statement. Flaws can always be found, and there is no dearth of flaw finders roaming the earth.

The best one can do is to apply techniques that are sound and reasonably having the least known bias, given the sample sizes.

In the present case, all samples were by definition small, and small samples place extra burdens on veracity. The situation is unavoidable since typical Thoroughbreds do not run many races in their careers, let alone in one season.

They most certainly do not run thirty races on the same track, at the same distance, under the same surface conditions and carrying identical weights – all in a single year. Such are the conditions that would be technically required to compare Thoroughbreds with minimum bias. It ain't gonna happen!

Fortunately, two salient facts emerged from this study which helped strengthen the conclusions derived. Each was totally unexpected.

The first was that most of the data points regarding run time versus distance were distributed along nearly perfect straight lines. Perfect, in this context, means that the horses' trend lines generally matched the data with over ninety-nine percent accuracy.

The lowest COD, in fact, was 0.9100 for John Henry as a 5YO. Even that value is considered an extraordinarily good fit of trend line to data in any research area. It was the lone exception for this study at such a low level.

The Low COD was due to seven of his twelve races being at 1.5 mi and his corresponding times approaching a non-normal distribution. The SD for these seven races was 6.28, and such a wide spread adversely affected the COD of the fitted trend line.

The general trend lines were so nearly perfect that it seemed each horse had a kind of internal autopilot reminding them to increase speed just enough as distance increased so that their trend line would remain linear.

This does not mean, contrary to a possible misconception, that the trend lines must be wrong because constant speed is required to achieve this result.

On the contrary, if one calculates the corresponding speeds for increasing distances by simply dividing the distance run by the corresponding time, one will find that speed does decrease steadily as distance increases. This is expected since we know neither human nor animal can maintain a fast pace regardless of distance run. Common sense dictates as much, and the linear trends substantiate this.

For example, Citation's average speeds as a 5YO drop from 56.81 ft/s for 6 f to 55.47 ft/s for 8 f and eventually to 53.57 ft/s for 16 f. These results are calculable directly from his LTA. His data points grace his trend line nearly like a perfect string of beads, and yet his speed decreased by 5.7 percent for the distance covered by his trend line.

The second serendipitous fact regarding the DRFC data was that most of the run time distributions, where they could be tested, were normal.

The Shapiro-Wilk test can be used on samples of size as small as three. About eighty-eight percent of the 2YO's data and eighty-five percent of the 3YO's data tested normal using the Shapiro-Wilk criterion supplied by Lumenaut® for Excel.

Had the run time distributions from the LTA generally proved non-normal, then the results of the LA would have been suspect.

Secondary Purpose

A second purpose of this study, naturally following upon successful completion of the first, was to approach a settlement of controversies amongst Thoroughbred aficionados regarding comparisons of horses such as Man o' War and Secretariat.

Ample, substantiated data were presented in that endeavor so that the fair-minded person could make a reasonable judgment about which "Big Red" was really more talented.

When the statistical dust settled from the data runs and simulations, the conclusion – hinted at before it was explicitly stated – was that there was no single greatest horse of the past century, certainly if one requires such a horse to have competed in consecutive years from juvenile to mature adult.

There is one exception to the above statement. That exception is the Hungarian-bred filly, Kincsem. As the previous chapter showed, Kincsem competed at ages two through five. She was undefeated in all fifty-four career races.

She carried weights that would be considered unthinkable by modern standards. She ran distances few horses will or can run effectively. She competed against both colts and fillies, and she beat them all.

However, aside from Kincsem and restricting this study to the particular group of Thoroughbreds chosen by BHI Inc., plus six selected horses, one finds outstanding horses representing a single age group but none which covers the four major ages at which Kincsem competed.

Secretariat came closest to that distinction by scoring the highest combined points for the 2YO and 3YO levels.

The statistical analyses used herein on Daily Racing Form data allowed advantages regarding plate weight and track condition to horses racing before 1950.

Those analyses show that sixteen horses (with one tie) stand as top candidates for greatest horse honors amongst their respective four age groups.

One might refer to these final top candidates as the Sweet Sixteen, a catchy epithet favored in other sports.

Alphabetical Listing: the Top Candidates

First Flight, Landaluce and Ruffian, were the leading candidates for best Thoroughbred, colt or filly, as 2YOs.

Cigar, Easy Goer and Secretariat were the top 3YO candidates.

Spectacular Bid, basically true to his trainer, Grover (Bud) Delp's claim, may tentatively be said to be the best 4YO ever to have looked through a bridle. "The Bid" lead in total points over four other 4YOs, but the tally was close.

The best 4YOs were: Affirmed, Dr. Fager, Seattle Slew, Spectacular Bid and Swaps. This was an interesting and, indeed, closely matched set of great champions whose final points ranged from 176 to 211.

Finally, for the 5YO and last group analyzed, the top contenders were: Cigar, Citation, Forego, Noor and Skip Away.

The greatest hiatus in rankings between this study and the BHI panel results undoubtedly concerns Ruffian and Noor. BHI ranked them thirty-fifth and sixty-ninth, respectively.

In reality, for their particular age groups, they should be ranked near the very best of the best, based on the results of this analysis.

It is assumed that because BHI was attempting to select a single greatest horse based on overall career they were forced to make tradeoffs. Certainly it appears that they underrated Ruffian's record at both ages two and three and Noor's at age five. That Kincsem was nowhere in the BHI picture is, interestingly, obvious.

The present study indicates that Secretariat was not a candidate for the greatest as a 2YO nor was Man o' War a candidate for greatest either as a 2YO or 3YO!

Of course BHI also overlooked horses like First Flight, La Prevoyante and Optimistic Gal. I conclude that, in keeping with Mr. Bill Nack's observation, if there was folly afloat anywhere in their rankings, it was in these myopic misjudgments.

The 5YO age group was considered a good place to stop because it represents full maturation for a horse and because it would be nearly a pointless exercise to do analyses up to and including the thirteen-year-old group, the oldest recorded age at which a horse, Grey Lag, was listed in the BHI rankings.

Since that group is a set containing one element, few could argue that he was not the greatest 13YO of the past two centuries! But few probably care about that.

Other Considerations

Does this book, as its title alludes, truly settle the controversy about Thoroughbred greatness?

As in all of life, two contradictory answers immediately arise: "yes" and "no." Hopefully there is also room for "maybe."

The controversy is nearly settled for those whose favorite horse was chosen as candidate for best in one of the age groups. Being a candidate always leaves room for further discussion. For others, a resounding "No!" is the answer.

It does not matter to some, however, that rigorous logic and strict adherence to scientific protocol was followed in determining these results.

A segment of people simply will not and do not wish to follow logical analysis to its conclusion. Or, just as likely, they choose to believe that the person determining the conclusions must have some hidden agenda or other he was promoting, or that he made egregious errors.

They will spend hundreds of hours searching for reasons why the data were mishandled or misrepresented.

Seven reasons bearing on these charges were, in fact, discussed previously in the text.

I, however, am satisfied that no basic statistical stone was left unturned in being eminently fair to each horse considered for these analyses, given the available data.

There are also those who will say that the sample of size fifty is inadequate. I offer the following rebuttal-explanation.

First, the entire BHI set of 100 was not chosen because it would not have made statistical sense, not because the author wished to eliminate, for instance, Ta Wee, who happened to fall eightieth on the BHI list, but because the BHI panel itself felt competent enough to place Ta Wee that low. One could argue that a sample of fifty is too small, but the line must be drawn somewhere. Based on the results derived herein, the entire sample of 100 would not have changed the basic conclusions.

Second, this study admittedly focused on North American Thoroughbreds as *candidate greatest* horses – not as *the greatest* horse. Thus, ample room remains for personal preference and future study or debate.

Third, if a sample containing complete data on every Thoroughbred since Eclipse were possible to obtain, and though it were analyzed to the nth degree on the latest Cray or IBM computer, objections would still abound. Such is human nature.

Finally, as my maternal grandmother Reid liked to say, "Enough's enough, and too much is plenty!"

It would have been indeed surprising if the BHI panel members were so inept that all their selections were, for example, inverted and that the present study really examined the worst rather than the best available records!

Therefore, fifty being considered well beyond a large statistical sample, it was felt that this gave at least the top North American Thoroughbreds of the past century-and-a-fraction ample chance to pit their records against each other.

This contention was basically supported by the initial data sort which reduced the competitors, as 2YOs and 3YOs, to twenty and ties.

It was noted earlier that a high percent of the top BHI ranked horses actually *were* in the top ranking of the data sort, although in a modified order.

This was not accidental and should help lead skeptical readers to conclude that the sort, although artificial to some extent as are all such sorts, was basically fair and sound. It contained, in other words, parameters relevant to racing ability, which is all one can ask.

No single parameter is a perfect bellwether of racing ability.

From the sort, the data of the remaining 2YO and 3YO horses were subjected first to Linear Trend Analysis (LTA) and finally to Three-Sigma or Limits Analysis (LA).

The data analyses for the 4YOs and 5YOs were limited to LTA and LA without first sorting because extended analyses, such as including additional data sorts, would only detract from the main interest group over which people argue Thoroughbred greatness – the three-year-olds.

That they are the focal point of equine discussions is undoubtedly due, as discussed, to the popularity of the Triple Crown, with all its implications of Olympian proportion and immortality. Only three-year-olds are eligible for that grail.

In reality, obviously, the horses themselves do not contemplate greatness. They do not worry whether humans have placed them in the Thoroughbred Hall of Fame or in other hallowed shrines.

I'm quite certain that Secretariat did not miss a night's sleep wondering whether the ESPN panel would vote him among the top 100 athletes of the 20th century, as it did (thirty-fifth) near the century's end. Since no other non-human received that distinction, this should also tell reflective readers something regarding further comparisons.

Horses may have some equivalent of an "equine high" surge through them when they stare malignantly, á la Seabiscuit or Dr. Fager, at an opponent before kicking into high gear and leaving him in their dust, but beyond that they are serenely and blessedly removed from the realms of human bickering created to lend spice to life or to attempt defining something that is ineffable by its very nature.

A Tale of Two Big Reds

A final word is in order, however, for fans of the most touted Thoroughbred of the entire twentieth century, Man o' War.

There is little doubt that he was one of the great Thoroughbreds of all time, certainly of his "era" – the first two decades of the past century.

And, although it may not appear thus from the results herein, it was not the author's intent to diminish his achievements in any manner or to tarnish the luster of his name. I too am taken by the legend of the first "Big Red."

However, even with liberal time adjustments to each of his 3YO running times, his LTA indicated that he would have been distinctly slower between 0.75 mi and 1.5 mi than Secretariat.

Only at 1.625 mi, or 13 f, the uppermost distance included for 3YOs, would Man o' War's trend finally have bested Secretariat's time.

Recall again that the trend lines of these top Thoroughbreds generally have extremely close fits to their respective data, well above 99 percent.

Regarding both Man o' War and Secretariat, their trend lines fit the data to over ninety-nine percent accuracy. More precisely, the trend lines for both have nearly identical CODs of 99.4!

This is unbelievably close to a perfect mathematical straight line. Additionally, since the CODs are equal in their cases, one cannot say that the trend of one horse is more or less accurate than the trend of the other and that they cannot be directly compared. That argument does not hold statistical water. Both fit their data equivalently.

Travers Considerations

As a final remark on this topic, consider data from the Travers. It is the oldest continuous race in America, a prestigious 10-f contest held at Saratoga, New York since 1864 – as the Civil War still lingered over the land.

In 1920 Man o' War ran the Travers in a time of 121.80 s.

The average time for the entire decade of the 1920s for that race was 126.24 s.

Thus, Man o' War's time was 4.44 s faster than the average for that decade!

Now consider this – the average time for the Travers during the decade of the 1970s was 121.72 s. This means that Man o' War's time was a mere 0.08 s slower than the average time for the decade fifty years later.

I ask the reader to consider that this leads to at least two salient conclusions. First, it implies that Man o' War was genetically unique for his time and that he was already equivalent to horses racing a half century later.

Second, it means that the Saratoga track conditions of the earlier era were essentially equivalent to the era of the 1970s.

If they had been distinctly inferior when Man o' War ran, he would have been unable, or extremely unlikely, to have posted such a time.

Since the average running time of the Travers during the 1970s decade was 121.72 s, this means it was 4.52 s faster than the average time of the 1920s.

About eighty-seven percent of this time difference (3.93 s) is explainable by the power curve representing increases in foal crop size versus simultaneous decrease in Travers running time over the twentieth century, as is now shown.

Chart 24 displays the decline in average running time for the Travers from the early to the late twentieth century. Notice that it agrees with similar curves presented earlier for the Triple Crown races and for the Santa Anita Derby. It indicates that changes in foal crop are a major determiner of changes in average decade running times.

Chart 24
Travers Decade Times vs Foal Crop Changes

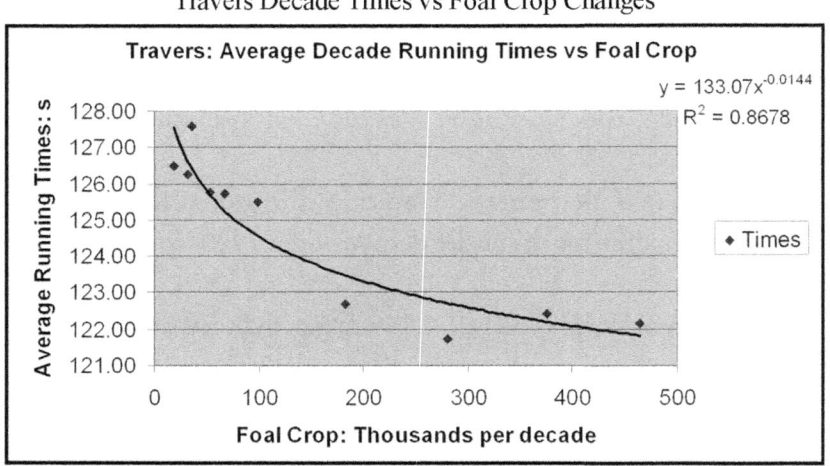

These facts strongly imply that, at most, 0.59 s could be due to a combination of plate weight and track effect on Man o' War's running time for the Travers in relation to the 1970s decade.

By contrast, Secretariat's LTA indicates that he would run a typical 10-f race in 120.41 s. This average is predicted with 99.4 percent accuracy by his LTA.

If 0.59 s is subtracted from Man o' War's 121.80 s, the remainder is 121.21 s. Secretariat would thus still have won an average 10-f match against Man o' War at Saratoga by a predicted difference of 0.80 s had they met repeatedly as three-year-olds.

Closing Thoughts

All readers should consider one additional fact that is generally completely overlooked regarding Secretariat's racing style.

He preferred to run behind the field for a major fraction of the early part of his races. If one reviews, for example, only the Kentucky Derby and Preakness films, he is seen to begin sweeping *around* the entire field somewhere near the clubhouse turn.

Mrs. Chenery, his owner at the time, said he learned to do this because he was "mugged" in his maiden race of Tuesday July 4, 1972 at Aqueduct. He wanted, after that experience, to stay clear of the field.

Now realize that the turns at Churchill Downs are one-quarter of a mile around while those at Pimlico are three-eights of a mile around.

This means that, for the Kentucky Derby, Secretariat ran *at least* 96 feet farther (about twelve lengths) by staying *at least* fifteen feet from the rail for both turns as he passed the field.

In addition, it is easily calculated from basic trigonometry that he ran about eleven feet extra (1.4 lengths) from his number-ten post position while bearing in to near the rail and the rear of the field during the opening seconds of the race. This was illustrated in Figure 3.3. These extra distances total 107 ft, or about 13.4 lengths.

Therefore, instead of running a straight 6600 ft that comprise 10 f, he actually ran 6707 ft, at minimum. Watch the time difference this makes!

Dividing the longer distance by his official time of 119.4 s, one finds that he would have been at least 1.90 s faster had he actually run 10 f. Thus, his winning time for the Derby over Sham would have been 117.49 s, rather than 119.4 s the record books will forever show.

At his *actual average speed* of 56.17 ft/s, he would have beaten Sham by over thirteen lengths instead of by the officially listed 2.5. Remember that this estimation is based upon a minimal approximation for rail clearance.

In other words, Secretariat and his partner Ron Turcotte repeatedly ran races in a manner eschewed by John Loftus, Man o' War's rider for his juvenile season.

Loftus was hesitant, even at the sprint distance of 6 f at which Upset handed Man o' War his solo loss in the Sanford, to swing around a field of six other horses for fear of using too much of his horse's energy.

This hesitation, it is argued, cost Man o' War that singular career loss.

Besides further highlighting the extraordinary ability of Secretariat, all this leads to what I believe is an appropriate remark with which to approach a denouement on the entire subject. It is a now-famous quote by sportswriter Rick Bozich of the Louisville-Courier Journal.

It carries as much import now, in light of what has just been discussed, as when first penned --

"Never insert Secretariat's name in the same sentence with the Derby winner until at least two more races have been run!"(28)

C8

Let us gladly applaud and revere, each as our temperaments and sensibilities may allow, the sixteen truly incomparable horses of the four age categories that finished highest in this study.

And let us stand totally in awe of Kincsem, that special filly from Hungary, for the marvelous feats she performed on foreign soil. She may, indeed, be the Greatest Horse of All. All other personal favorites aside, she has my vote.

And, all somewhat frivolous questions of greatness aside, it is appropriate that all the horses herein selected may reside for many years as the standards against which racing excellence is judged.

Each is truly their own unique reference point.

In the last analysis, however, only God holds the true measure of the creatures He summoned from the south wind those countless eons past.

EPILOG

To every thing there is a season, and a time to every purpose under the heaven;
-- Ecclesiastes, 3:1

In attempting to perform an unbiased analysis of Thoroughbred racing data, I have always been aware that it is impossible to please all the people all the time, to paraphrase Abraham Lincoln.

In fact, if one could please all people, one would end by saying precisely nothing valuable.

My real hope is that I have been entirely true to the great spirits of the magnificent creatures we humans call Thoroughbreds. It is them I fear offending more than anyone.

I also hope that, in the most literal sense, they are meeting daily in a better world entirely removed from time, whatever precisely that is, and that they run free and unencumbered by the artificial barriers we humans heap upon their flesh – all for amusement.

It does me good to imagine Man o' War sidling near to Secretariat and saying, "C'mon, buddy, feel like running today? Maybe we can go over there and convince Ruffian, Barbaro, Ferdinand and Exceller to join us. That should be a blast!"

We humans owe these creatures who perform at our bidding our greatest respect. We do not always afford that and certainly do not extend the stewardship to them as we were charged by the prophet Moses nearly 3,500 years ago.

It is good to recall, even occasionally, that we are not the masters of creation we pretend to be.

All civilizations eventually crumble. All return their atoms to their lowest energy levels – more prosaically called "dust." We are no exception to the law of universal heat death.

As it is much better writ,

"I said in my heart, after the speech of the sons of men, that God has chosen them out, but only to see that they themselves are but as beasts; that that which befalls the sons of men befalls the beasts; even one thing befalls them both: as the one dies, so the other dies; yea, they have all one breath; so that a man has no preeminence over a beast; for all is vanity. All go to one place; all are of the dust, and all return to dust.

Who knows whether the spirit of man goes upwards, and the spirit of the beast goes downwards to the earth?"

-- *Ecclesiastes 3: 18-21*

ABBREVIATIONS USED

Average/Mean: Av; also x_{av}

Blood-Horse, The, Inc.: BHI

Coefficient of Determination: COD; also R^2

Colt: A male foal; a male equine through age four

Daily Racing Form, Champions: DRFC

Feet/Second: ft/s (unit of speed)

Feet/Second-squared: ft/s^2 (unit of acceleration)

Filly: A female foal; a female equine through age four

Five-Year-Old: 5YO

Foal: A newborn equine, male or female

Foot: ft

Four-Year-Old: 4YO

Furlong: f (one-eighth of a statute mile; 660 ft)

Gelding: An altered male

Horse: A male equine upon reaching age five

Juvenile: A colt or filly, age 2

Kinetic Energy: KE

Linear Trend Analysis: LTA

Mare: A female equine upon reaching age five

Mile or statute mile: mi (5,280 ft)

Momentum: mv; also p

Pound: lb

Second: s (1/86,400 of a day)

Shapiro-Wilk Test: S-W

Sophomore: A colt or filly, age 3

Standard Deviation: SD

Standard Error of Estimate: STEYX

Three-Sigma-Analysis/Limits Analysis: TSA/LA
Three-Year-Old: 3YO
Two-Year-Old: 2YO

REFERENCES

1. The Blood-Horse, Inc., *Thoroughbred Champions: Top 100 Racehorses of the 20th Century*; Lexington, KY, 1999

2. Daily Racing Form LLC, *Champions*; Daily Racing Form Press, New York, NY, 2000

3. Sowers, Richard, *The Abstract Primer of Thoroughbred Racing*; Old Sport Publishing Company, Stockbridge, GA, 2004

4. Cahill, Thomas, *The Gifts of the Jews*; Nan A. Telese/Anchor Books Doubleday, New York, NY, 1998

5. The American College Dictionary; Random House, New York, NY, 1958

6. Armstrong, Geoff and Thompson, Peter, *Phar Lap*; A Sue Hines Book, Allen & Unwin, Crows Nest, NSW 2065, Australia, 2003

7. Sowers, Richard, Personal Communication; November 30, 2007

8. Daily Racing Form LLC, *The American Racing Manual 2005*; Daily Racing Form Press, New York, NY, 2005

9. http://en.wikipedia.org/wiki/Momentum

10. Ainslie, Tom, *Ainslie's Complete Guide to Thoroughbred Racing*; Third Edition, Simon & Schuster, New York, NY, 1986

11. Kinney, Ed, Email correspondence concerning steel vs. aluminum shoes; March 16, 2001 and June 24, 2006

12. Hollingsworth, Kent, *The Kentucky Thoroughbred*; The University Press of Kentucky, Lexington, KY, 1985

13. Gershwin, George & Ira, *It Ain't Necessarily So*, Porgy & Bess, 1935

14. Davidowitz, Steven, *Betting Thoroughbreds: A Professional's Guide For the Horseplayer*; E. P. Dutton, New York, NY, 1977

15. Equineonline.com, *Annual North American Registered Foal Crop by Decade*; 2006

16. Hopkins, J. Michael, Executive Director, Maryland Racing Commission; Email communication, June 19, 2007

17. Sykes, Bryan, *Saxons, Vikings and Celts: The Genetic Roots of Britain and Ireland*; W. W. Norton & Co., New York - London, 2006

18. Information Please, *Time Almanac 2005*; Pearson Education, Needham, MA, 2005

19. Schmuller, Joseph, *Statistical Analysis with Excel for DUMMIES*; Wiley Publishing, Inc., Hoboken, NJ, 2005

20. Woolfe, Raymond G., Jr., *Secretariat 25th Anniversary Edition*; Raymond G. Woolfe, Jr. with Piedmont Publications & Graphics, Warrenton, Va, 1998

21. http://www.stcroixforge.com/products/specifications

22. Cottam, Paul, Email correspondence dated May 1, 2001

23. Ours, Dorothy, *Man o' War, A Legend Like Lightning*; St. Martin's Press, New York, NY, 2006

24. Scanlan, Lawrence, *The Horse God Built*; Thomas Dunne Books, New York, NY, 2007

25. Kapper, Don, Progressive Nutrition, Beach City, Ohio, Email correspondence dated August 22, 2007

26. Hillenbrand, Laura, *Seabiscuit: An American Legend*; Random House, New York, NY, 2001

27. Sowers, Richard, *Shatterproof: The Most Unbreakable Records in Sports and Why*; Old Sport Publishing Company, Stockbridge, GA, 2005

28. Bozich, Rick, Louisville Courier-Journal, May 23, 2000

INDEX

CODA

What, then, is time? I know well enough what it is, provided that nobody asks me; but if I am asked what it is and try to explain, I am baffled.

St. Augustine of Hippo
Confessions; (A.D. 397-398)
Book XI; Verse 14

Rather than love, than money, than fame, give me truth. I sat at a table where were rich food and wine in abundance, and obsequious attendance, but sincerity and truth were not; and I went away hungry from the inhospitable board.

Henry David Thoreau (1817-1862)
Walden, 1854
Chapter 18 "Conclusion"

CB

Printed in Great Britain
by Amazon

83232777R00144